Harry Thomas'
MEMORY LANE
VOLUME III

RHYL ＆ PRESTATYN
VISITOR

A COLLECTION OF HARRY'S PICTURES & STORIES FROM THE
RHYL & PRESTATYN VISITOR NEWSPAPER COLUMN, MEMORY LANE

Also available: Harry Thomas' Memory Lane, Volumes I & II
More Local History Books available at www.gwasg.com

ISBN: 0-9550338-2-9
© Printed & Published in November 2005
by Gwasg Helygain Ltd
68/70 Kinmel Street, Rhyl, Denbighshire LL18 1AW
Tel: 01745 331411   Fax: 01745 331310
info@gwasg.com   gwasg.com

All rights reserved. No part of this book may be reproduced or transmitted in any form or by any means, electronic or mechanical, including photocopying, recording, or by information storage and retrieval system, without the written permission of the Publisher except where permitted by law.

Introduction

Welcome to Memory Lane Vol III, the latest book in this series. I am very happy that the Visitor column and these books continue to be so popular. So many of you contact me through the newspaper contributing facts and photos for my records and I thank you all for your invaluable contributions.

It was when I was gathering my thoughts for this intoduction that I chanced upon the following verse, which seemed to be a fitting introduction to my latest book. Happy reading!

We met and married a long time ago.
We worked for long hours when wages were low.
No T.V., no wireless, no bath, times were hard.
Just a cold water tap and a walk down the yard.

No holidays abroad. No carpets on the floors.
We had coal fires and didn't lock doors.
Our children arrived, no pill in our days;
And we brought them up, without any state aid.

They were safe going out to play in the park.
An our old folk were safe going out in the dark.
No Valium, no drugs, no L.S.D.
We cured all our ills with a good cup of tea.

No vandals, no muggings, there was nothing to rob.
We felt well off with a couple of bob.
People were happier in those far off days.
Kinder and caring in so many ways.

Milk men and paper boys would whistle and sing.
A night out at the pictures was our weekly fling.
We had our share of trouble and strife,
We just had to face it, that's the pattern of life.

Now I'm alone, I look back through the years.
I don't think about bad times or troubles and tears.
I remember the blessings, our home and our love.
And that we shared them together,
I thank God above.

Author Unknown

Harry Thomas
November 2005

I am continually looking for additions to my archive and would be interested in purchasing all types of old picture postcards, old local china, souvenir items, local cine film and also viewing or copying items of local interest. If you have anything that might be of interest please don't hesitate to call me on 01745 - 889773.

Foreword

RHYL PRESTATYN VISITOR

Welcome to Volume Three of Harry Thomas's Memory Lane, a compendium of his ever popular features of the same name that appear weekly in the Rhyl, Prestatyn and Abergele Visitor newspaper.

It doesn't seem five minutes that Guto from Gwasg Helygain approached me to see if the idea of chronicling Harry's writings in book form for the first time was a viable idea, of course the paper readily agreed and now the release of the Visitor Memory Lane books are fast becoming a regular fixture in the calendar for local historians and those with an interest of they way our locality has changed over the decades.

Perhaps Harry's work is taking on a new dimension as the new millennium enters its sixth year with both Rhyl and Prestatyn changing their image drastically. In Rhyl the much vaunted promenade Drift Park will radically alter the appearance of our seafront as will the image of the town's fast growing High Street change with the arrival of new department stores and shopping developments.

In Prestatyn, alterations are underway in lower High Street with major demolition work paving the way for the eventual arrival of a new Tesco store, a controversial project that has divided opinion but draws a united front when it comes to the way the look and feel of this most traditional of communities will present itself.

Whatever happens, you can be sure Harry will be there to record it and eventually, when the dust settles, his writings will remind us of the way we were before these changes and we will probably bemoan the fact that 'things were better before…'

The fact, however, is that things weren't always better and progressive change is inevitable in this fast-paced, stressful, society we live in. We must all face and embrace change but with the cushion of nostalgia to remind us of the way we were, and that's where the likes of Harry come in.

The local historian will always have a huge role to play in any community and Harry is up there with the best, his devotion to times past is legendary and his efforts are enjoyed and respected by a huge number of people, young and old.

That is why I am delighted that my paper continues to associate with and work alongside Harry and Gwasg Helygain via his Memory Lane column. I trust you enjoy this book and will look forward to another volume of the same this time next year…see you then!

Mark Jones
Production Editor
The Visitor Series Newspapers
November 2005

Acknowledgments

I am indebted and more than grateful to the following for their more than generous contributions and for those of you who had to endure my harrasement during the complation of this book: the Directors of Gwasg Helygain Ltd; Eddie, Linda, Sian & Guto Lloyd-Davies for their enthusiastic, invaluable and ceaseless support in the publishing of this book. Fred Hobbs, Vivien Hughes-Davies, DW Harris, Arthur Dilks, Dorothy Chard, Olive Gardner, Ken Vickers, Bertha Davies, Mary Calland, Gwyneth Parker, Michael Lewis-Jones, Gwynedd Parry, Chris Mellor, Janet Otley, Robert Scott, Ivor Davies, Cynthia & Dennis Jones, Merion Thomas, Derek Bond, Lisa England, Mike McKeown, Ruth Pritchard and the Lowry Centre.

This book is dedicated to those most treasured in my life: Harry Thomas Jnr, Emma Thomas, Mark Tyldsley, Jayne Ruby McGibbon & Alana May.

A special mention also to Jenny & Hazel Walker.

In memory of Wendy C Thomas.

Harry Thomas
November 2005

Avenues and alleyways

The postcard on the right is of Maes-y-Groes, (field of the cross) Prestatyn, looking towards High Street from Eden Avenue in 1923. The parish church spire (built in 1863) dominates the skyline as a very welcome landmark.

The house on the left, once known as Latrigg, was sold for £50 in 1850 and was one of the more popular boarding houses in Prestatyn during the late 1930s.

It was run by Francis and Leonard Pearse ("Save with Dave's" parents) and there were so many guests during the summer that there were three sittings for breakfast, dinner and tea. Today this building has been converted into a private three-house complex.

When the Prestatyn to Dyserth railway passenger service was introduced between 1905 to 1930, there was a passenger halt established at the end of Maes-y-Groes, however the name of the halt and Maes-y-Groes had to be changed to Chapel Street (Bethel Chapel is at the entrance to Maes-y-Groes), due to the fact that holiday makers requiring the use of the halt were finding it difficult to pronounce and ask directions to Maes-y-Groes.

It reverted back to its former name when the line closed in 1930, notice the Chapel Street name on the postcard!

Tradition tells that there once existed in Prestatyn, an important Roman Catholic settlement, and Maes-y-Groes may have been one of those sacred sites where a cross or shrine was erected for the convenience of passing pilgrims to perform their religious devotions.

It is also interesting to note that in the early 1900s, ED Jones of Olive Villa, Meliden Road, had a workshop on the corner of Maes-y-Groes (the building behind Hafod Memorials today). His unusual trade was Bardic chair and coffin maker.

The postcard on the left is of Sandy Lane, Prestatyn in the 1930s looking towards the Victoria Hotel from the entrance to where Gwelfryn is today, the former site of the fondly remembered 69 Club, demolished in 1987.

The trees on the right were planted in 1904 on land near the railway-bridge and in 1951 a preservation order was placed on them. The railway-bridge itself was erected in 1897.

During the early 1900s Sandy Lane became renowned for chimney fires and it was Prestatyn's PC Nelson who had to deal with complaints, after being told that "Sandy Lane was like a London fog", with houses permanently covered with soot both inside and out.

Open all hours for the shoppers' convenience

Long before the arrival of supermarket shopping, High Street grocers provided all the essentials needed for the shoppers in the community.

One such High Street grocers in Prestatyn was the popular shop of John Meredith Hughes, grocers, bakers and confectioners, pictured here in 1910 (today these premises are occupied by Blockbusters Video).

John Hughes who lived above the shop with his family is seen in the doorway in the top photo with his son Edward.

The shop had the distinction of selling food of the highest quality. On offer at his shop were tins of Princes' lobster and crab, the best Danish butter, the choicest cured York ham, quality cheeses and bara brith which he baked freshly himself in his bakehouse at the rear of the shop.

For a small fee of 1/6d (8p) or 2/- (10p), a horse-drawn delivery service to the door was in use for customers (bottom picture).

John Hughes also owned a small general store in Newmarket called "Siop Ganol" (middle shop). He subsequently sold his shop in Prestatyn in the 1950s to Coopers, a small grocery chain and retired to live in Pendre Avenue, Prestatyn.

A bit of sauce with your stick of rock

For the holiday maker and the day tripper, their summer months visit to the seaside resorts along the North Wales coast have always had a "happy times are here at last" feeling.

Since the early 1900s when rail travel boomed and made North Wales seaside resorts readily accessible, holiday makers and day trippers have eagerly made their way to Prestatyn, Rhyl, and Llandudno, longing to escape from the tedious and claustrophobic work of factory life and the smoke and noise filled industrial towns and cities of the North and Midlands.

It was the beginnings of a one hundred year British love affair with the seaside resorts of North Wales.

The bucket and spade brigade flocked in their thousands to the North Wales resorts for a welcome escape or a few days or weeks to relish the delights and simple pleasures of the sun, sea, sand and embracing health giving ozone-filled salubrious sea air, and for the traditional "dip in the briny".

Seaside holidays also meant seaside comic postcards with their by-gone vulgar images poking fun at fat ladies, drunks, hen pecked husbands, courting couples and bikini-clad pretty girls.

After their suitcases were unpacked and they had crossed swords with the inevitable disagreeable landlady, on the following day holiday makers were visiting the newsagents and souvenir shops to purchase a handful of the sauciest comic postcards to scribble on the back a composed message ending with the most famous words in British seaside history "Having a wonderful time, wish you were here" and off they would be sent to relatives and friends with a furtive grin from the postman as he delivered them.

The comic seaside postcard, a British Institution, are increasingly recognised as important social documents providing valuable evidence of by-gone images of fashion, work, attitudes and a host of other facets of historical interest.

Comic seaside postcards are leaving us with a one hundred year legacy of making us smile, and anything which can do that in this day and age for so long can't be that bad, can it?.

For a while the traditional seaside holiday remained unchallenged until cheap package holidays became irresistible to many, but while the British sun shines, the seaside holiday will remain as popular as ever.

The seaside comic postcards on this page were on sale during the 1950s.

A school in mourning

The sayings that "every picture tells a story" and "a picture is worth a thousand words" were possibly written with old picture postcard in mind, as I have shown in past Memory Lane features and as the two postcards on this page illustrate.

The top postcard is of children from Bodnant School on Marine Road, Prestatyn, walking down the town's High Street in the late 1920s on their way to the parish church to attend the funeral of their late headmaster JH Jones. Teacher RH Edwards is the man in the trilby hat leading them.

JH Jones was known to be a very strict headmaster who always kept the pupils in line with the cane. It is interesting to note the school fashions of the day - the boys in their caps and the girls in their bonnets.

The popular and fondly remembered Teague's café seen on the left, is today an empty shop that was previously Threshers off-licence. The gas lamp stood outside Bethel Chapel.

In those days, Prestatyn Town Council employed lamplighters who travelled the town with a lighted taper on the end of a pole, igniting the mantles of the lamps every night and going round again in the early morning to put them out. These men were paid four pounds, 10 shillings, (£4.50) a year!

Electricity came to Prestatyn when the formal inauguration of electric power took place in 1927. It was switched on by councillor Clement Hughes, chairman of the Electric Company.

The bottom postcard looks up Prestatyn High Street in 1938, from where Charles the Butchers is today.

The car on the left is parked outside Parsonages, one of the most noted eating establishments in Prestatyn in those days, who served lunches, grills, afternoon teas and also sold the most delicious, freshly made chocolates and confectionery (I can almost taste them now!).

Today these premises are the Principality Building Society. They were previously Diskos.

Tom Brooks, who ran a garage in the town known as Prestatyn Motors, where Tegid O Jones Funeral Services are today, recalls as a young boy riding his bike to purchase batteries for his bike lights at one of the shops in the High Street.

On coming out of the shop he got on his bike, parked on the pavement nearby, and as he was halfway up the High Street he realised he had got on the wrong bike!

It must be remembered that in those days cycling was a popular pastime, with half the population of the town in the possession of a bike, and cycles left unattended did not have to be locked. Trusting times they certainly were – where have they gone? Note the abundance of bikes in this scene!

Two superb social history picture postcards that positively do tell a story.

Looking back at the best days of our lives

A picture gallery of old school photographs continually delights and holds considerable interest and charm for readers of the Memory Lane column. And for those of you who take great pleasure in recognising old school friends, here is another selection of old school photographs for your scrutiny, we wonder where they all are now!

The top photograph shows some of the characters that have passed through the corridors of Prestatyn Clawdd Offa school in the 1960s.

Back row, standing from left to right are : Brian Lewis, Vernon Egerton-Jones and Phil Williams. Back row sitting l-r : David Evans, David Owen, Tony Allit, Peter Gregory, Kenny Stevens, R C Jones, David P Owen, Brian Holmes and Phil Stanley.

Front row sitting l-r : Clive Morris, Noel Cambell, David Hughes, Michael Holiday, Martin Lodge, Stuart Maybury, Phillip Wharton, Gerald Lumsden, Brian Jones.

Clawdd Offa School opened on September 6th 1956, the first headmaster at the school was Dan Owen, and the school was designed for 620 pupils. When it opened on the Tuesday it was said to be already overcrowded. Today the old Clawdd Offa is known as Prestatyn High School.

The bottom photograph was kindly donated by Gwen Owen of Penyffordd and is of Ffynnongroyw CP Infants School, Mornant Avenue, pictured in 1948.

Back row l-r : teacher Miss Jones, Gwyn ?, Gwynn Jones, Alan Harrison, Raymond Parry, Raymond Williams, Edmund Roberts (passed away in 2001),Tommy Owens (known as " chips", parents ran the chip shop in the village).

Middle row l-r : unknown, unknown, Glyn Thomas, Edith Jones, Eirlys Thomas, Dorothy Latham.

Front row l-r : Maureen Stockton, Pamela Dennis, Margaret Davies, Rita Parry, Eirwen Parry, Gwen Roberts, Nan Jones (passed away in 2003).

In those days due to lack of space the school children at Ffynnongroyw CP Infants had to walk to Moriah chapel schoolroom at the other end of the village for their school dinners.

Booming Businesses on Busy High Streets

Before the growth of the coffee and milk bar phenomenon, Lyon's Corner Houses were among the places you could go for a cup of tea or coffee.

Staffed by waitresses in black uniforms Corner Houses were quite elegant with bands playing, and you had to be seen to leave once you had drunk your tea or coffee and paid your bill.

When the first coffee and milk bars were opened, they were hugely successful. Subsequently the bars provided a meeting place for people of all ages to sit and talk in a relaxed atmosphere and meet like minded people. In this way the coffee and milk bars started a social revolution.

Fortes were possibly the most popular coffee and milk bar bars in North Wales throughout the 1940s, 50s, 60s and 70s where friendships and relationships were forged over an espresso coffee or knickerbocker glory.

Decorated in pastel shades of pink and green with Lloyd Loom tables and chairs, Prestatyn's Fortes (pictured above in 1985) was run by the ever-so-friendly and cheerful Francesco Forte (known as Frank) and Joan Walters who later became his wife. Frank's brother also ran a Fortes in Llandudno.

The light refreshments comprised; espresso coffee, a diverse selection of flavoured ice-cream sundaes, knickerbocker glories, banana splits and their deliciously famous home-made Eccles cakes made by Mr Forte and his baker Ifor Bradshaw in the backroom kitchen while Joan was kept busy with the hissing sound of the espresso coffee machine.

A nearby neighbour whose upstairs flat overlooked Fortes kitchen recalls on warm moonlit nights listening to Frank Forte's Italian voice through the open skylight window uplifting her as he sang Back to Sorrento and other Italian and English songs, as he baked those famously delicious Eccles Cakes.

A notable dish, when in season, was strawberries, tasting so delightfully different that Joan was frequently asked what she added to enhance their flavour. When asked, she would give a furtive smile but never divulged her secret ingredient. This was discovered years later when a customer chatting to Mr Forte asked what the secret ingredient was. With a laugh he told her it was "white pepper, and that's our little secret" he told her.

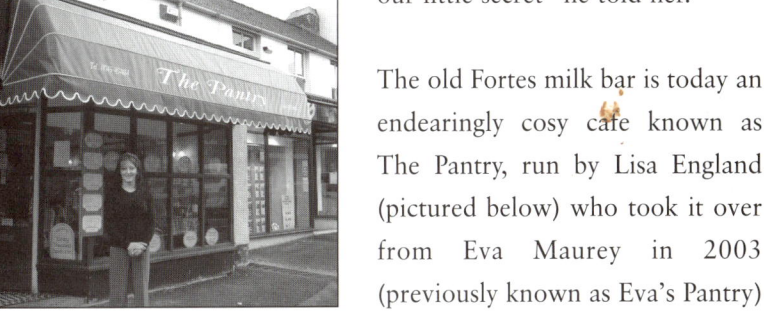

The old Fortes milk bar is today an endearingly cosy cafe known as The Pantry, run by Lisa England (pictured below) who took it over from Eva Maurey in 2003 (previously known as Eva's Pantry) where regular customers savour the delights of the cafe's homely atmosphere and relish the exemplary menu of home-cooked meals and cakes, freshly baked on the premises.

Well known celebrities are known to call in at the Pantry when visiting Prestatyn, one regular is legendary snooker player Jimmy White who visits the Pantry for a full breakfast when playing at Pontins.

Vestiges of the time, harking back to the days of Fortes can still be seen at the Pantry in that the Lloyd Loom tables and chairs are still in use at the cafe to this day.

Holiday park once held German POWs

Arthur Lee founded Merseyside Holiday Camp in a field at the foothills of Craig Fawr in 1909, its foremost purpose was to provide a short holiday for the poor children from Birkenhead and District.

A considerable amount was spent on the camp's timber construction which consisted of many well catered for facilities comprising separate dormitories for sleeping accommodation, a spacious dining hall, indoor covered swimming pool, games room and an extensive playground with an assortment of swings, slides, swing maypole and roundabouts.

The first arrivals at the camp were 100 children from Birkenhead and district who arrived at the camp on July 9th 1909.

On their arrival the children were given strict instruction not to wander or play close to the old mine workings nearby due to the danger of falling down one of the mine shafts.

A once-a-week treat for the children was a visit to a sweet shop in Prestatyn, they were at one time a regular sight on the road seen walking in an orderly line down from Meliden to Prestatyn.

For most of those underprivileged children their short holiday at the camp was a new and great discovery for them, which they thoroughly relished.

However, one or two children who, at being far from home and at unfamiliar surroundings for the first time in their young lives, became homesick, as the message on the bottom 1954 postcard reveals, "Dear Mum, Please bring me home, having a rotten time. Love Bill XXXX".

At the end of their stay at the camp the children were said to have gone home looking healthier and happier than when they arrived.

During the First World War (1914-18) the camp was used as a German prisoner of war camp under military guard. During the day the German prisoners worked on the farms in the locality for which they were paid six shillings (30p) for a 10 hour day, they were allowed only a small amount of this for their services. The prisoners were not allowed on the roads to and from the farms without an armed guard military escort. They were found to be good and willing workers and their behaviour was said to be quiet and polite.

By 1918 there were 20 prisoners at the camp and on their arrival back at the camp from the farms at 7pm lights would be out at 9pm when they would be locked in their rooms.

A doctor would attend to the prisoners for dental treatment and for teeth extractions, the dentist would be forgiven for giving that extra pull! At the end of the war the prisoners at Meliden were sent back to England to be repatriated to Germany. Many of them didn't want to leave as they had been well treated by the local farmers and villagers who appreciated their hard work.

In 1991 the multi-million pound Craig Park Country Club and Hotel was built on the site of the old Merseyside Holiday Camp. A corner of Meliden that once held fond memories for those poor and underprivileged children from Merseyside.

Top photo: Children and staff pictured in 1934 at two of the dormitories at Meliden's Merseyside Holiday Camp.
Bottom: The spacious dining hall at Merseyside Holiday Camp, pictured in 1954.

Preparing for The Great War

There was no shortage of volunteers in the First World War. Men rushed to recruiting offices in the belief that the war would be over in three months. Boys who were under age attempted to enlist rather than be left out and miss what to them was an exciting adventure.

For military purposes the military authorities commandeered Rhyl's vast number of boarding houses for the billeting of soldiers. Daily, hundreds of soldiers were seen drilling, training and being inspected by their superiors along the length of the promenade. Soldiers were also seen marching through the town, backwards and forwards from parades and military exercises.

Many of these smartly dressed soldiers arrived here from South Wales and comprised the Rhondda Battalion and the South Wales Borderers.

Many brave Rhyl soldiers lost their lives in the Great War and the wounded who arrived back home filled the wards of the Alexandra Hospital and the Men's Convalescent Home in Bedford Street, which was used as a Red Cross Hospital (today this building is used by various charitable organisations).

When the Germans sank the passenger liner the Lusitania in 1915, there was a strong public outcry against the Germans in this country resulting in a German barbers in Queen Street being attacked by a small crowd with stones thrown through the barber's shop windows.

The outcome was a fortunate one for the barber in that he executed a hasty escape and was never seen again. I assume the German barber's name was "Mein Herr Cut!"

The top postcard shows an inspection of the 2nd South Wales Brigade by General Sir Ivor Phillips on Rhyl prom in 1915. Rhyl's Pavilion Theatre creates a striking backdrop to the whole event (the Sky Tower is located here today).

The bottom postcard shows soldiers from the Cheshire Brigade marching along Wellington Road in 1914 (alongside today's narrow gauge railway station. Sydenham Avenue is seen in the background). They are en route to their camp in a field near the Foryd.

A message in fountain pen on the back of this postcard to an M Bennett in Congleton, Cheshire, reads: "Dear Maria, we have had a rough time today, we marched about 6 miles with full dress and did it make us sweat. Love from Harold xxxx."

Ghostly goings on in Bodfor Street

It is doubtful if any ghost story in Rhyl or the neighbourhood has been more documented and authenticated than that of the "Bodfor Street ghost".

The apparition takes on the form of a man in a shirt and trousers but not wearing a jacket that has been seen in the early hours of the morning crossing the road to Conrad's stationers (formerly Hadley's) as if to post a letter , then he disappears!

One of the most authenticated and vivid sightings of the Bodfor Street ghost occurred some years ago.

A policeman on duty at two o' clock in the morning turning into Bodfor Street from the Police Station in Wellington Road, suddenly noticed the figure of a man in the doorway of the old Card Cabin (today the Del-it-Ful sandwich shop seen on the right hand side of the photo above) the figure then crossed the road towards the direction of Hadley's stationers (today renamed Conrad's seen on the left hand side of the photo above).

Without loosing sight of the figure, the policeman followed it into the doorway of Hadley's, took the torch off his belt and shone the light into Hadley's doorway only to be confronted with an empty space, the figure seemed to have disappeared into thin air.

Astonished at the disappearance of the figure the policeman shone his torch on the dry floor of the doorway, but could see no foot prints despite the fact that it was pouring with rain.

When the policeman came off duty and disclosed his experience to his colleagues, he was not met with disbelief at his story as he had expected. He later discovered that the the figure he had seen was that of the Bodfor Street ghost, which over recent years had reportedly been sighted by many local residents and also by policemen of long service in Rhyl, who had for years walked the beat in Bodfor Street.

It is reputed that the figure was for many years a resident of Bodfor Street and met with a violent death by his own hands. Before doing so he had posted a letter in a wall-type post box, long since removed following alterations to Hadley's frontage which was previously known as Sandoe's commercial stationers and high class leather goods.

Are the sightings of the Bodfor Street ghost no more than imagination, or was the untimely death of this man a tormented spirit that is to eternally replay his actions of posting a letter before his death?. There have been numerous sightings in recent years, sadly lack of space does not permit me to document them here.

Remember me to your mother

Lynda Pritchard of Tan Lan was to encounter such a vivid haunting experience that it was to later bring shock and disbelief to her mother.

Lynda, a happy and intelligent teenager, lived with her mother, brother and two sisters in their modest home in Tan Lan on the coast road between Talacre and Point of Ayr.

She left the house on that particular warm summer's afternoon in July to see her friend Lynnette who worked at the garage near the Totem Pole Café on the coast road Gwespyr (pictured above).

Passing the Totem Pole Café, Linda saw her old next door neighbour Mr Simon standing on the front lawn of his new home, next door but one to the café. Lynda greeted him with a friendly hello to which he replied: "hello Lynda, remind me to your mother!"

Lynda thought nothing more of her meeting with old Mr Simon and continued her walk to the garage to see her friend, where they talked for a while before Lynda started to make her way back home.

A couple of weeks passed when a conversation between Lynda's mother and the boy next door by chance happened to be on the subject of ghosts.

For some reason which Lynda still can't explain to this day, she said to her mother: "By the way, mum, I saw Mr Simon a couple of weeks ago and he told me to tell you that he was asking for you."

Lynda's mother abruptly replied: "When did you see him?", Lynda's mother gave a nervous laugh and continued "Don't be daft Lynda, he's been dead since January."

Lynda replied with a positive tone in her voice: "I saw him as clearly as I'm standing here talking to you."

Lynda's mother explained, with the blood visibly draining from her face, that Mr Simon had suffered a fatal heart attack whilst putting the rubbish out and was found dead by the dustbin some time later.

Today Lynda lives in South West London and her mother has since passed away, but Lynda still vividly recalls her experience that summer's afternoon all those years ago, when she saw the ghost of Mr Simon.

Above: The very popular and excellent Totem Pole Restaurant with owner David Jenkins standing in the doorway.

Before the days of superstores

The forerunners of the grocery chain shops, such as Irwin's, the Star Supply Stores, E B Jones, Masons and the Maypole, were the small and unrivalled family grocers shops which thrived in our towns and villages in the early 1900s onwards and supplied the everyday household needs of families.

Distinctive by their advertising slogans and goods which embellished their shop fronts, the most important people, the customers, predominately females, were never neglected.

A study of what the customers purchased in those days would reveal some interesting social attitudes, for instance, was there a touch of " upstairs downstairs" about the lady asking for a pound of best bacon and a pound of kitchen bacon? Or the working class customer asking for the three pennyworth (one and a half pence) of bacon bones for making a tasty broth.

Pre-packed goods, refrigerated food and self service were unheard of and the goods were sold from sacks, barrels and tins. Tea, sugar, flour, salt, biscuits, butter and other household goods were weighed then wrapped when bought.

Fresh bread sold in the shop was baked in the bakehouse at the rear of the premises, and butter had to be patted into shape with small wooden paddles before being wrapped. Bacon was freshly sliced on a machine and cheese was cut into portions with a slicing wire.

For the convenience of the customers, the family grocer, who was always dressed in a white apron, would provide wooden chairs in the shop while their orders were made up and errand boys on bicycles carried parcels in brown paper securely fastened with grocers knots for those who wanted goods delivered.

Before the advent of electricity, one regular shopping item was a seven penny (three and a half pence) packet of candles as they were a necessity for home lighting.

Paper money in those days was rarely seen and shopping was paid for in five shilling pieces (25p), half crowns (13p), florins (10p), shillings (5p), sixpence's (3p), and threepenny bits (one and a half pence).

The family grocers became legendary for their service and courtsey, in an unhurried and friendly shopping environment, qualities that have sadly disappeared from today's rushed and queue burdened supermarkets. Perhaps they could learn from their forerunners regarding customer care!

Top Postcard - Standing tall : Grocer Thomas Lewis stands in the doorway of his shop Gerlan Stores in Marine Road, Prestatyn in 1929. the shop was named Gerlan, as his wife came from a village of the same name near Bethesda. Today, the premises are occupied by Accent Software and La Belle Femme, beauty salon. Thomas Lewis also owned a shop in Llanfairfechan called Gwalia Stores.

Bottom postcard - A study in history: A superb social history study as William Brothers grocers shop staff and errand boys pose outside the shop at the top of High Street, Prestatyn in 1905. Today this building is occupied by Pizza Cottage.

Picturing Rhyl in days gone by

The leisurely quaintness of a long-gone by-gone day in Rhyl is faithfully captured on the top postcard as a horse and carriage idly journeys down the High Street on a summer's day in 1918, when the pace of life was less hurried.

The strikingly impressive building on the right where Boots the Chemist is today, was known as Magnet Buildings. Among the traders here were Wills Jones Magnet, studio photographer; Mr Eisiski, tobacconist; the Star Supply Stores and the Constitutional Club.

The shop on the right with the blinds next to Magnet Buildings is Garson Allen gents outfitters, high grade tailor, clothier and hatter.

The shop seen next door is Stacy, run by a Miss Stacy who sold jewellery and fancy goods.

Today, these premises are occupied by Clinton Cards, the Card Factory and H Samuel.

Opposite Magnet Buildings and these two shops, nearby the gas lamp on the left at the time was the town's Post Office, when the cost of sending a first class letter was one old penny (half a penny) and the cost of sending a postcard was half a penny.

The gas lamp on the left was not in use due to the fact that electric lighting was installed in the streets in 1901.

The bottom photograph shows Garson Allen's shop and staff, gents' outfitters, high grade tailor, clothier and hatter, pictured here in the 1920s following alterations to the frontage of the shop in Rhyl High Street.

Welsh links of a matchstick man

During the early 1960s, Mike McKeown of Prestatyn who was 14 at the time and an Army Cadet at Prestayn's Royal Artillery Cadet Force also attended meetings of the Army Cadet force at Rhyl, frequently having to spend time on Prestatyn's Railway Station to await his train to Rhyl.

And it was throughout those numerous moments on the station at Prestatyn that his attention would be drawn to an elderly man in a beige raincoat carrying an old-style open-top Gladstone bag, who on seeing Mike greeted him with a friendly "hello". Mike politely replied with a friendly "hello" in return, and they both engaged in conversation. Mike recalls him saying that he had been around the town of Prestatyn and that he sketched and painted.

Inquisitively Mike asked him where he had come from and his answer was that he came from around about Salford in Manchester.

On another occasion while Mike was on Prestatyn station awaiting his train to Rhyl to attend his Army Cadet meetings, he once again saw the same friendly elderly man, this time with a sketch pad, sketching and smiling whilst looking in the direction of Craig Fawr, Meliden.

Mike also recalls seeing the elderly man again standing by the walls of the old Penisardre farmhouse and looking up the High Street whilst sketching on small pieces of paper with a pencil and crayon, (16th century Penisardre was sited where the shopping precinct is today and was demolished in 1964).

It was only when Mike saw a documentary on television at the time he realised that the friendly elderly man he had seen sketching and had talked to was Britain's best-loved artist, LS Lowry.

Mike subsequently joined the Royal Corps of Signals and became a radio man. Today he lives in Prestatyn and treasures those valuable memories of the days he saw Lowry sketching in Prestatyn.

Born in 1887 LS Lowry is famous for his "matchstick" men paintings of England's industrial North West which snap and crackle with passion and commitment. But he is known to have spent many a happy holiday in North Wales and to have pencil sketched scenes of Prestatyn, Rhyl, Rhuddlan Castle, Flint and Denbigh.

Lowry died in 1976 at his home in Elms in Longdendale, Cheshire.

In November 2004 a 1929 sketch of Edward Henry Street, Rhyl and an oil painting of the Foryd Harbour, Rhyl, by Lowry were among 20 drawings and paintings up for auction at Christie's auctioneers, London. Denbighshire County Council wanted to buy the Lowry scenes for Rhyl Library and Museum, but sadly were unable to obtain the funding.

The Edward Henry Street, Rhyl 1929 sketch sold for £22,000 and the Rhyl Foryd painting for £75,000.

Opposite: One of Britain's best loved artists, LS Lowry.

Above: 1925 Pencil sketch of Prestatyn by LS Lowry.

Below: Mike McKeown pictured on Prestatyn Railway Station in 2005 where he had observed Lowry sketching during the 1960s.

Dances in days of respectability

Happy times and unforgettable memories when well known Prestatyn dance teacher Ivy Kay held her very popular fancy dress nights and sequence dances at Prestatyn's Royal Lido (today's Nova Centre) came flooding back for Mary Calland of Ferguson Avenue, Prestatyn.

Mary recalled with affection that the fancy dress nights and sequence dances were well attended and always packed out and everyone had the time of their lives.

Mary remembers that the foxtrot, waltz and palais-glide were the favourite dances of the day.

The old-time and modern dance music was played by Rod Williams and his dance band, who Mary recalls were a great favourite and widely known in Prestatyn, Rhyl and the neighbourhood as they played in many of the local dance halls of the day.

Rod Williams was recognised as an excellent piano player and was church organist at Mostyn's Parish Church.

By day Rod Williams ran his village grocers shop at Kidderminster House, Ffynnongroyw with his staff of three women, Phillis Jones, Nancy Tinman and Priscilla Rowe.

Along with her husband Eric, Mary Calland ran the successful Prestatyn School of Motoring from 1954 up until 1986 and recalls that during the week nights in the 1960s, modern sequence dancing was also held at Prestatyn's Conservative Club rooms in Eden Avenue.

Mary fondly remembers those special occasions at the Lido when sequence dances and fancy dress nights were also held at Easter and each year at the Lido's Christmas party.

We each have those special memories of memorable great nights out over the years. For me it was those many sensational nights at Pat and Colin Swallow's Palace in Rhyl then on to the Twisted Wheel Club in Manchester, but that's another story.

Mary Calland and her friends remember those wonderful nights at the Lido when the world had different thoughts and values and respectability was a word inbred; nevertheless, they certainly did have the time of their lives.

My very grateful thanks to Mary Calland for donating the original photographs on this and the opposite page to my archives.

Opposite page: Smiling faces at Old Time Music Hall with Ivy Kay's Sequence Dance Group at the Gronant Institute 1964. The women were a picture of beauty in their dresses, Mary Calland is seen in a stunning white dress second from the right, as is well known local singer Kath Bell of Gronant in a white dress with flowers, fourth from the right. Rod Williams and his dance band are seen on the stage in the background.

Above: No prizes for guessing who's wearing the most stunning costume in this picture at Ivy Kay's fancy dress night at the Lido in 1965. Left to right, Mary Calland, Barbara Cashen, Ethel Cashen, Olive ? and Pat Johnson.

A horse-drawn holiday haven

A delightful "unhurried" tranquil portrait of a day long gone by it is faithfully captured on the postcard above. This view is looking down Wellington Road from the corner of Russell Road and High Street in the summer of 1906 (looking from where Oxfam is today).

The Town Hall in the background had been dominating the town's skyline since it first opened in 1876.

As early as 1898 pioneer cinematographer Arthur Cheetham was showing films every month at the Town Hall.

They were films which Arthur filmed himself of local events, which included Rhyl May Day, A Football Match At Rhyl, Irish Mail Train Passing Through Rhyl Station, A Minstrel Show at the Happy Valley, Llandudno and The Arrival and Departing of Trains at Llanfairfechan Station.

It is interesting to note that Arthur Cheetham was showing his films at the Town Hall only two years after the very first showing of moving pictures in Paris by the Lumiere Brothers in 1896.

Prior to the advent of motorised transport, horse-drawn vehicles were the only form of transport on the roads of Rhyl in 1906 when this photograph was taken.

At the time, horse-drawn vehicles were not apt to causing traffic hold-ups.

Today the peace and tranquillity on the roads of Rhyl has disappeared with the horse-drawn vehicles, only to be disturbed by the noise of the permanent flow of traffic that streams through the town today (bring back horse-drawn vehicles!).

The right corner building on the postcard above once belonged to Hughes the Tailors. Established in 1863 they were once one of the oldest family businesses in Rhyl (today this building is occupied by Discount Books).

The shops and businesses along this part of Wellington Road when this photograph was taken were, Parr's Bank, Mr Gunner Bootmaker,

Sheffield's Ironmongers, Emlyn's Library, Mr Slinn, Boot and Shoemaker, J Beech, China and Glass Dealer and the Birmingham Arms.

The photograph above is strongly reminiscent of the past and is a superb social history document from a bygone day in Rhyl, showing Jesse Beech, his wife and children, posing for this photograph outside his china and glass shop in Wellington Road in 1893 (today these premises belong to William Hill).

Opposite page: Less hurried days in Rhyl looking down Wellington Road in 1906 from the corner of Russell Road and High Street (where Oxfam is today).

Above: Jesse Beech with his wife Elizabeth Beech nee Hope. Standing beside her mother is Mary Elizabeth Hope Beech, in the cart are Francis Jesse Hope Beech and Gladys May Hope Beech pose for this endearing family photograph outside their shop in Wellington Road in 1893. Elizabeth Beech was the daughter of Edward Hope, he was one of Rhyl's earliest residents. He went on to become the Market Hall Inspector on his land that later Hope Place was built. Jesse Beech's old shop is today the premises of William Hill.

Search ends in emotional visit

A chance meeting in Prestatyn High Street with Cynthia Jones of Prestatyn, whom I knew from the days when we both lived in Gwespyr, led her to find her grandfathers grave after many years of searching.

Cynthia's grandfather James Hayes was born in Mostyn, lived with his wife Sarah at Halendy and fought in Gallipoli, Turkey in the First World War.

Cynthia's mother had always thought her father was buried in Turkey, but Cynthia was to discover that this was incorrect and that was the reason her grandfather's grave was never found.

Following many wrong leads, Cynthia had come to yet another dead end in her quest to discover the location of her grandfather's interment during the First World War.

In our conversation, I advised Cynthia to contact Hawarden Record Office, which she did and was told by the very helpful staff there that she would find the information she required by searching the Commonwealth Graves Commission website.

It would be an understatement to say Cynthia was elated when she found the website and the information she had been searching for, for so long – the location of her grandfather's grave, which was on the Greek island of Lemnos.

Cynthia had discovered that her grandfather had been shot in the leg, taken to a field hospital on the island of Lemnos and later sadly died of dysentery (a disease that induces inflammation of the intestines, at that time an incurable disease). He was only 37 when he died.

When the soldiers of Mostyn came home on leave, Cynthia's grandmother had waited in high spirits outside her door in Halendy for her husband to arrive home on leave, not knowing he had died. On seeing soldiers from Mostyn passing she shouted to them "Have you seen Jim?", they shouted back in a friendly gesture that they hadn't, but they knew that he would never return home and that his wife Sarah had been left a widow with six children.

Over the next few exhilarating days Cynthia resolved that she was to visit her grandfather's grave in Lemnos, not only for herself and her family but also for her 92 year old mother Elizabeth who had been only two years old when her father died.

Cynthia and her husband Dennis subsequently flew out to Lemnos and hired a taxi to the military cemetery at Portianos. Within minutes at the cemetery Cynthia had found her grandfather's grave – in an emotional and tearful moment. The trip closed a valuable and important chapter in Cynthia's family history.

While they were at the military cemetery, Cynthia's husband Dennis discovered the headstone of Gunner JE Jones of Newmarket.

Opposite: James Hayes of Halendy, Mostyn, the First World War soldier who lost his life and is buried in one of the Commonwealth graves in the island of Lemnos. His grand-daughter Cynthia Jones, today lives in Prestatyn and made a poignant visit to his grave.

Above: Demolished in the 1960s, Halendy cottages as seen here looking towards Holywell in 1905, the road just off the postcard to the right is the hill leading up to Rhewl.

Below: The headstone of Gunner J E Jones of Newmarket. Are there any relatives in the neighbourhood who know of this soldier, buried at the military cemetery in Portianos?

Scouting for its first recruits

On October 28th, 1914, under the presidency of R M Hughes MP, a meeting was held at the Town Hall, Rhyl for the purpose of forming a Rhyl branch of the Boy Scouts Association, as the Scout movement had at that time been recognised by the government.

Subsequently 50 boys enrolled to become Rhyl Boy Scouts, with another 50 ready to become members.

The historic rare postcard above captures the very first members of the recently formed Rhyl Boy Scouts, pictured outside Rhyl's Town Hall with their new uniforms in 1914. The poster in the background is advertising Gay Spirits at Rhyl's Pavilion Theatre.

The Carnegie Free Library seen above the door to the entrance of the Town Hall (which can still be seen there today) was opened in 1907 through the support of a donation from an application to the Andrew Carnegie Trust from Rhyl Council.

To qualify to be a member of the lending library you had to be over 10 years old and no-one under the age of 14 was allowed in the reference room without the appropriate permission from the librarian.

The Boy Scout Movement originated with an experimental camp through means of Lieutenant Baden-Powell on Brownsea Island, Poole, Dorset in 1907.

Twenty boys were invited to try out the new " Game of Scouting" of whom nine were members of the Bournemouth and Poole Boys Brigade companies, and the remainder were the sons of Baden-Powell's own friends.

They were formed into four patrols to carry out a range of activities that included observation, woodcraft, cooking and swimming.

There were no uniforms, but under Baden-Powell's command the boys wore shorts- unusual for the period- and a badge based on the north point of a compass.

Town Hall, and Free Library, Rhyl.

It was not Baden-Powell's intention to establish a national youth organisation, but to provide guidance for boys who wanted to train themselves in frontier skills that he himself had learned in various parts of the Empire.

From that very first meeting 91years ago to establish a scouting movement in Rhyl, the scouts are still going strong in the town with their headquarters today based at Ty Newydd Road in Rhyl.

As early as 1898 pioneer cinematographer Arthur Cheetham, whose gramophone shop was the first shop in Rhyl to be lit by electricity, was showing his hugely popular films every month at the Town Hall. They were films which Arthur filmed himself of local events which included, Rhyl May Day, Rhyl Town versus amateurs football match, EH Williams Merrie Men (Pierrots) on Rhyl sands, and an Irish mail train passing through Rhyl station.

Thankfully to Arthur Cheetham, many of his films have survived today. They capture an invaluable document of Rhyl's history rich past.

Opposite: the very first members of the Rhyl Boy Scouts in their new uniforms pictured outside the Town Hall in Rhyl in 1914.

Above: The Town Hall pictured here in 1909 was opened at a cost of £8,000 in 1876 to provide an administrative centre for the town.

Birth and death of a coal mine

Coal mines have always been an indication of a community's social history, and Point of Ayr Colliery near Ffynnongroyw was one of those coal mines strongly associated with the community and its families, who relied directly or indirectly on the pit for their living.

The first bore holes were sunk at Point of Ayr in 1865, but there were many engineering and geological difficulties to overcome. It was not until the 1880s that the first top quality coal was produced by men who had toiled for years at Point of Ayr in the search to discover those rich seams of coal under the Dee Estuary.

In those early days the coal was brought to the surface with the help of pit ponies which were used underground to pull the heavy-laden coal carts.

By 1922 half of Point of Ayr's output of coal was being shipped to northern and southern Ireland, the Isle of Man, the breweries on the island, and to Prices Patent Candleworks at Port Sunlight by coal carrying boats, the Talacre, the Point of Ayr, the Tan Lan and the Clwyd.

At the time of the miner's strike there were 31 pits employing 22,000 men in Britain, but a 125 year industrial heritage was about to change forever when on March 1st, 1984 the Coal Board announced the closure of Yorkshire's Cortonwood Colliery. The miners saw that the government's policy to close its uneconomic pits as a threat to their jobs, livelihoods and families, and they subsequently became united in a national "walkout".

By March 1st, 1985, the NUM voted for a mass return without a settlement. At Point of Ayr 84 miners out of approximately 700 stayed out on strike to the bitter end.

The closure of Point of Ayr Colliery in 1996 signalled the end of an era and consigned coal mining in North Wales to the history books. The coal industry that Wales had become famous for had come to an end, when coal was known as black gold.

Opposite: A huge blast and the end of an era for Point of Ayr as a poignant moment is caught showing the 98ft winding shaft seconds from crashing to the ground, toppled by explosive experts in 1997.

Above: Picketing miners under observation by police during the miner's strike at the entrance to the Point of Ayr Colliery in 1984.

Below: The closure of Point of Ayr colliery for coal production in 1996 signalled the end of the mining industry and consigned coal mining in North Wales to the history books, Point of Ayr is pictured here in 1992.

The miners strike photo is courtesy of Jeff Pitt. The Point of Ayr and winding shaft photos are courtesy of Terry Williams. The pictures on this page were kindly donated to my archives after they were taken.

Cinema role for a delivery man

One of the most familiar and instantly recognisable sights on Britain's roads for many years were the lorries and vans belonging to Coopers Furniture Removers and Carriers of Prestatyn, who delivered furniture, parcels and a host of other items up and down the country.

This noted Prestatyn firm was founded by Bill Cooper in the 1930s, who came from humble surroundings in Bury, Lancashire, to reside at Victoria Road, Prestatyn to establish his successful fleet of delivery vehicles.

Bill Cooper is no longer with us, neither is his once thriving and esteemed delivery service which regrettable came to an end in the middle of the 1980s. But one man who has happy memories of working with Cooper is Ivor Davies of Central Avenue, Prestatyn.

In an engaging lengthy discussion, Ivor went on to recount that he started working for Coopers as a delivery hand in 1946 at a wage of fifteen shillings a week (75 pence).

Ivor also recalled that Cooper's also ran a taxi service, a fleet of tipper wagons for haulage and a fleet of delivery vans all based at their depot in Bastion Road, Prestatyn (the old depot has today been converted into office units).

With a work force of over 30, including mechanics, drivers and delivery men, Ivor told me that Coopers also transported Prestatyn's football team around North Wales and they also changed into their football gear in one of the larger vans they were transported in.

Ivor recalls that Cooper's were the first in the district to acquire articulated lorries, and during the 1940s these large lorries were only allowed to travel at a maximum speed of 20 miles per hour.

Ivor frequently went along to help deliver furniture on these huge lorries which often travelled as far as Ireland or Scotland and with the speed limit so low it usually took a few days to travel there and back, so they stopped for bed and breakfast which in those days Ivor recalls was 10 shillings and six pence (53p).

Ivor also remembers one of his first trips on one of the articulated lorries to Blaenau Ffestiniog, and that the lorry had just been painted by local signwriter Stan Merick and on returning to the depot the newly painted lorry had been badly scratched and damaged by overhanging branches and hedgerows which, in those days were not cut back as they are today. As you can imagine, the boss, Bill Cooper, was not very pleased. But he was a generous man as he treated his staff every year to a day out in Blackpool, as "we were one big happy family" Ivor recalls.

An amusing incident Ivor remembers was the time friends, family and residents of the town were stopping him in the street to shake his hand and to ask him for his autograph. Bemused by all this attention, Ivor subsequently discovered that his fame was due to a Coopers advert which they had been screening at the Palladium Cinema (where Boots the Chemist is today), which Ivor had not seen and had no knowledge that the film in which he appeared was to be shown at his local cinema.

As I got up to leave following Ivor's memorable reminiscences, I couldn't help turning to him with a smile to say, "Ivor, have you time to give me and autograph".

Above: One of Coopers large articulated lorries for furniture removals pictured in 1946, left to right, company owner Bill Cooper, Jim Cooper and Ivor Davies. A familiar sight on Britain's roads for many years were the vans belonging to Cooper's Furniture Removers and Carriers of Prestatyn, pictured opposite in the 1950s. When these vans were in a large town or city unloading furniture or delivering parcels, people would see the name on the side of the van and say to the delivery men, " Oh, we have been on holiday to Prestatyn!"

Old coins caught a rogue postman

At a time when many of the colourful and characterful antique and collectable shops that once adorned our towns and villages are closing and a large number have long since disappeared, the Rhyl Coin and Stamp Centre has maintained a constant stream of customers.

It opened its welcoming doors 20 years ago at 12 Sussex Street, four doors from where it is today at its new and larger premises in 4 Sussex Street, opened at the end of February 2005 by local MP and postcard collector Chris Ruane.

The move to larger premises was due to expanding stock, thriving business and because the old shop was to be demolished as part of the old indoor market regeneration. A welcoming personal service with a smile and a hearty conversation from Bruce, Marco and Mike is part of the Coin and Stamp Centre's success, along with the wealth of fascinating items on sale, which comprises jewellery, old and new, old bank notes, old postcards, coins, stamps and a host of collectables.

The Coin and Stamp Centre was founded by Colin Rumney in 1980, and when Colin retired Bruce Goulbourne took over the business in 1986 and has since gone from strength to strength.

Due to the shop's allurement and the diverse merchandise on sale, the Coin and Stamp Centre has naturally attracted its fair share of rogues and villains over the years.

One incident that made the headline news in the local papers in recent years happened as the owner Bruce Goulbourne provided a mail service for coin collectors, and it became unfortunate that a dishonest postman had been opening the packages intended for the coin collectors. But the postman made the mistake of attempting to sell the coins to the Rhyl Coin and Stamp Centre, unbeknown to him that this is where they had originated!

The postman was subsequently arrested, dismissed from his job and dealt with severely by the courts.

To celebrate the Queen's Jubilee in 2002, Bruce Goulbourne sent a gift of a Welsh gold ring to the Queen. In appreciation he received a letter of gratitude from Buckingham Palace and today Bruce awaits with anticipation that follow-up letter decreeing his shop "By Royal Appointment!"

For those of you who are dedicated collectors or are just fond of browsing, there are also other superb collectors shops in Wellington Road, Rhyl – Curio City, the Glory Hall and Nick Nax. These shops are emblematic of a bygone era of the traditional collectors shop – visit and experience a treasure trove of collectables. The welcoming doors of Aquarius Antiques in Market Street is also well worth a visit.

Photographs of the way we live today are valuable and important to us all and future generations as they capture tomorrow's history. The pictures on this page are the perfect illustrations.

Opposite: The new premises of the alluring Rhyl Coin and Stamp Centre opened by local MP Chris Ruane in February 2005.

Above: Marco & Mike at the old Rhyl Coin and Stamp Centre, 12 Sussex Street, now demolished as part of the old indoor market regeneration. At one time these were the premises of Pullers of Perth Dry Cleaners.

Changing face of High Street

The old postcard views of Prestatyn pictured here were taken at a time when two-way traffic was in operation through the High Street, it ceased being two-way in 1964.

Not everyone approved of the one-way scheme and there were public meetings held, and more than 3,000 people signed a petition to have the traffic flow altered to go down instead of up the High Street.

However, the council adhered to its decision but agreed that Clwyd Avenue should become one-way. The new bus station was also opened in 1964, by the then mayor Harold Crabtree.

The postcard above is looking up Prestatyn High Street in 1938 from the corner of Penisardre Road and from where the Royal Bank of Scotland is today, in the days when Prestatyn had a sense of pride in its achievement of having two cinemas, the Scala and the Palladium, when a visit to the cinema drew long queues and the films played to packed houses.

The Palladium Cinema on the right was opened in 1924 and, by many locals, unforgivingly demolished long before its time in 1979, today Boots the Chemist is sited there.

Elise Hinton's shop on the left sold wool, cotton, needles, pins, knitwear and handicraft items, a busy and popular little shop in the days when knitting, needlepoint, patchwork and crochet were popular women's pastimes.

Jason's of Prestatyn and Reeds Rains estate agents occupy Elise Hinton's old shop today.

The bus in this picture looks out of place and must have been one of the last photographs taken of a public transport vehicle at a bus stop in the High Street. This Crosville bus operated on the Rhyl-Prestatyn-Dyserth-Rhyl circular service, it is seen standing outside where the Card Warehouse is situated today.

The postcard above is looking down Prestatyn High Street in the 1930s from where Charles the Butchers is today. The original Boots the Chemist building is seen on the corner of High Street and Nant Hall Road.

During the 1800s this building housed the town's Post Office and grocers until it was badly damaged by fire in 1899. A new and more modern post office was built in King's Avenue in 1915 where it still operates today.

Old postcards without doubt illustrate that every picture tells a story, therefore helping to preserve our valuable heritage and history by showing us a window in which we can view the past, that is important to us all and for future generations.

Above: Prestatyn High Street in the 1930s from where Charles the Butchers is today, the original Boots the Chemist building is today the Card Warehouse. The trees are on the land belonging to 16th century Penisardre Farm. It was demolished in 1964 – the shopping precinct is there today.

Opposite: Prestatyn High Street in 1938 from the corner of Penisardre Road and today's Royal Bank of Scotland, in the days when two-way traffic operated in the High Street. It ceased being two-way in 1964.

The essence of a thriving village

In his booklet A Historical Guide to Prestatyn, published in 1912, Thomas Edwards writes of Meliden; "This once busy little village was originally known as Gallt Melyd".

In the time of William the Conqueror (1066-87) Meliden was called Ruestock, the name derived by reason of the excellence and abundance of corn grown in the district.

A claim has been made that the name is derived from Bishop Melitus, Bishop of London, and also the British Saint Melyd, both are incorrect as Melitus was never in Wales and Melyd lived long anterior to the foundation of the church."

The origin of Meliden's name is surrounded in dispute, however, in view of this it is understood that it is conceived from the anglicised composition of Gallt Melyd (wooded hill of Melyd).

The postcard above was a onetime commonplace scene in the village and a way of life long since gone, showing coal being delivered in 1915 via horse and cart, by an employee of Meliden coal merchant, Richard Mather. The coal is being delivered to Penllan, a house still standing today opposite the Red Lion pub. The seven cottages on the left were known as Tai Cochion (Red cottages), as they were built of red brick instead of the customary limestone. Old Mr Roberts a noted village cobbler lived here, and while the menfolk of the village waited to have their shoes repaired, they would discuss with Mr Roberts their views on matters of the day. Tai Cochion were demolished in 1937, the Red Lion car park is here today.

The Parish Church is seen behind Tai Cochion, its earliest reference is contained in the Doomsday Book of 1086. Throughout the years the village of Meliden has succeeded in maintaining its identity to be an old, historic mining village with a strong sense of community and heritage.

The bottom photo shows Mather and Roberts Butchers together with the premises of Richard Mather Coal Merchant, Main Road, Meliden (today known as Ffordd Talargoch). Louisa Mather poses in the doorway where she was the butcher whilst her husband Richard ran the coal business. He was once mayor of Meliden. They traded until the 20s or 30s and later these premises were to become Hughes' grocers and greengrocers and later a bakery.

The views that capture the past

These previously unseen views of Prestatyn High Street bring the past vividly to life, capturing a cathedral-like quietness when the town slumbered peacefully and devoid of any transport (possibly a Sunday).

Prior to 1904, footpaths in the High Street were non-existent and people had to move swiftly to avoid horse-drawn vehicles and cyclists careering down the High Street. They were also hindered by the gardens that projected out in front of the houses and to avoid them, were forced to walk out into the the middle of the road. Pedestrians were also confronted with an unsurfaced High Street. As a result, the road was very muddy in the winter and in the summer, dust caused serious problems, choking everyone that walked the High Street, a tarred surface was laid in 1909.

The top postcard is looking down the middle of the High Street in the summer of 1909 from where Presents with a Difference is today. Hopwood High Class Caterer and Confectioner on the right was also a cafe that served luncheons and teas. During the 1930s and 40s, the upstairs of this building became a very busy and popular homely cafe known as Aunt Jayne's, run by a Miss Olive Pritchard (pictured in 1995, but sadly passed away in 2000). A cake and bread shop was situated on the ground floor.

Olive Gardner nee Pilling of Meliden has affectionate memories of working as head waitress in the family atmosphere of Aunt Jayne's during the 1930s and recalls that the cakes and bread were freshly baked in the bakehouse at the rear of the building. As head waitress, Olive received fifteen shillings (75p) a week, recalling serving customers with coffee at fourpence (2p), a cup with a cream cake at sixpence (2½p).

In recent years, Threshers Off Licence occupied this building and today it is being converted into a restaurant. Victoria buildings opposite are today the business premises of Fish-n-Bits, Gail's Kitchen Cafe and Hayes Travel Agency.

The bottom postcard is looking down the High Street from the corner of Nant Hall Road in the summer of 1912. The little boy with his arms around the grocer's verandah support is where the Card Warehouse is today.

The trees are on land where the 16th century Penisardre farmhouse once stood, it was demolished in 1964. Shops along here today include Alec Edwards, Contessa, Abbey, Serve-u-Rite, Rumours Cafe, Bugatti and Cumberlidge the Jewellers.

Recalling bank life

While on holiday in delightful Dyserth, Elita Boyd purchased a February 16th 2005 copy of the Visitor newspaper, and on returning home handed the paper to her father, Clive Boyd, with whom she lived in Redgrave, Norwich, and this prompted Clive to write me a letter and to enter my Memory Lane postcard competition. The competition featured an old postcard view of Queen Street, Rhyl, showing Parr's Bank which revived numerous happy memories for Clive as he worked in the building next door when it was known as the District Bank (Parrs and the District Bank amalgamated and formed the Westminster Bank in 1972).

In his evocative and captivating letter, Clive wrote that Nelson's Motors, next door to Parrs, later became the District Bank where he was a junior clerk from 1960 to 1966. Nelson's Motors sold motorcycles, bicycles and prams and had an extensive sports department. Note the old penny-farthing bike on the roof.

Clive recalls that there was a Bradley's gents outfitters opposite and District Bank and that Bradley's shop sign was spelt in large letters etched out on a mirror which ran the length of the shop window, which Clive says: "I'm sure wasn't planned as the angle of the sign proved to be very helpful".

The lower half of the bank's window, Clive recalls, was made from frosted glass which meant you couldn't see the street or pavement or the pedestrians from the inside the bank. If the doorbell rang when the bank was closed, the member of staff answering the door would first look out of the upper half of the bank window and see who was at the door by their reflection in Bradley's mirrored sign.

Clive remembers that the bank was very proud of their secret security device, and it was almost a disappointment that no-one was ever wearing a mask or brandishing a gun.

Clive also recalls that in those days a large proportion of the economy was cash-based and working men were still paid in cash.

During the summer, Rhyl in those days witnessed vast numbers of visitors who brought in an influx of cash to the area which found its way into the shops and was subsequently paid into the banks.

Clive also recalls, "there were times when our bank was so awash with money that we literally ran out of places to keep it. The strong room, safe, cupboards, shelves, drawers and boxes were overflowing, and at its extreme the staff were shuffling through notes on the floor, and it all had to balance at the end of the day".

"Securicor had not yet been devised and every Thursday we would bundle up surplus cash, wrap it up in thick white paper with string and red sealing wax, then plastered with blue stick on HVP labels (high value parcel). It would all be sent by post to head office."

"One junior female clerk and myself carried the parcels through the streets to the Post Office (pictured above in 1900) which was in the High Street in those days. The trips were made regularly every Thursday afternoon at 3.30pm; we must have been the softest target imaginable for a determined thief, and why we were never bumped on the head and the money stolen I shall never know".

Remembering life as a nurse in the 1940s

I was approached by regular Memory Lane reader, Bertha Davies of Prestatyn, who showed me a photograph of herself when she was a nurse at the War Memorial Hospital, Grange Road, Rhyl (demolished in 1983, and today the site of Memorial Court).

She was more than happy for me to include her photo in Memory Lane, as I explained that readers may recognise family or friends. Over a coffee, the delightful Bertha, captured my attention with her engaging and vivid recollections of old Prestatyn and told me that as a nurse during the 1940s, she worked from 7am until 9pm with two hours off, and one day off a week, for two pounds and 10 shillings (£2.50p) a month, which included a uniform and her meals.

She recalled that in those days, the hospital had 1 men's ward with 12 beds, and 1 female ward with 12 beds, a children's ward and nine private wards. She also recalled that there was a large garden at the front of the hospital and that vegetables were purposely grown for the hospitals kitchen and as Bertha told me, "we were very health conscious even in those days". And it looked to have had a beneficial effect on Bertha as she didn't look her years.

Above: Back in the old days: Rhyl War Memorial Hospital nursing staff in 1947, back row left –right, Sister EO Jones, Bertha Davies. Front row left-right, Laura Jones, Kate Roberts, Sister Ceinwen Roberts, the Matron at that time was ME Jones of Llanuwchllyn, Bala.

Below: The War Memorial Hospital pictured in 1916.

Another evocative photograph for Memory Lane came from Ken Vickers of Crescent Road, Rhyl, who invited me to look through an overflowing album of old postcards and photographs. I had met Ken previously when he had told me of his days as a cinema projectionist at the Plaza.

As I was looking through Ken's album the photograph on this page caught my eye, of Ken as bar manager at Rhyl's Dixieland in the 1970s on the corner of Sydenham Avenue and the promenade. After that, it changed its name to Brunels in 1975.

Ken said, "The Dixieland was known as Rhyl's singing, swinging nightspot, and when it opened in 1970, it became the first nightclub in Rhyl to obtain a late night licence".

Open from 7pm until 1am, admission, Ken recalled, was 15p to 30p depending on who was appearing on the night. Many famous pop groups of the day appeared at the Dixieland, including The Tremeloes, The Marmalade, Chicory Tip, Mungo Jerry and Acker Bilk.

Ken still had the original 1970s price list for drinks and it's jaw dropping reading – a pint of mild was 16p, bitter 18p, lager 20p, whiskey 15p and rum 17p. Was it any suprise, Ken told me, that the Dixieland was always packed on a Saturday night and was one of Rhyl's most popular nightspots? Happy days - hic!

Above: Dixieland staff are pictured here in 1971, they are left-right, Ronnie Nutt, Avril Malley, Ken Vickers and Jill Evans.

The spooky secrets of Henblas's past

On approaching the charm and cathedral quietness of the rural village of Llanasa from Gwespyr crossroads, you will be immediately struck by the impressive-looking building on the left known as Henblas (Old Hall in English), once the home to Dennis Vosper, conservative MP for West Flintshire, who died in 1968.

Henblas was built in 1645, at a time when horse-drawn vehicles were a common sight in and around the roads of this tranquil little village.

It is an intimidating-looking residence that on first observations appears to be home of a number of hauntings.

During the First World War, German prisoners of war were held at Henblas and it was during this time that many of them saw the ghost of an old woman who haunted the ancient residence.

When a new family moved to Henblas some years ago, one of the young daughters repeatedly requested to sleep on her own in the small bedroom above the front door.

Curious as to the reason why her young daughter would wish to sleep on her own and not be scared at night in such a large home, one day her mother asked her.

Her daughter's reply was a shock as she said that when she awoke in the morning, "there is a small woman sitting in the chair by the window smiling at me, I like her and want to sleep in this room so that I can be company for her".

The old woman sighted at Henblas was not the only ghostly figure seen at the Old Hall. Over the years there have been sightings of a ghostly coach and horses driven by an unseen driver passing through the gates to the entrance, and it is said to be the omen of impending tragedy for whoever sees it.

On a hot summer's day in 1960, a man came to stay on holiday with some friends at Treetops Caravan Park in Gwespyr, and, as the day was hot and pleasant, they had all decide to walk up to Llanasa to sample the beer at the Red Lion Pub, just around the corner from the Old Hall.

As they approached the village, the visiting friend had walked on ahead of his friends, as the thought of a cold pint of beer on such a hot day was uppermost in his thoughts. On reaching the entrance to the Old Hall, to his astonishment, he saw the ghostly figure of the coach and horses driven by an unseen driver passing through the gates.

When he entered the Red Lion, the visiting friend with a noticeable tremble in his voice asked the Landlord, "are they making a film here?". Observing that his face was ashen white, he replied, "not lately, why do you ask?". Still with a slight tremble in his voice, he told the landlord and his friends of the coach and horses he had seen passing through the gates at the Old Hall.

Some weeks later, the men from Treetops Caravan Park took another walk to the Red Lion and recalling their last visit, the landlord inquired where their other friend was. Their response was a sombre that "he had died shortly after returning home from his stay with us".

Bygone summer days of Prestatyn

A delightful glimpse of an idyllic, innocent and unhurried way of life on a summer's day on the roads of Prestatyn in the days of horse-drawn transport is vividly captured in the old postcard views pictured here. A graceful period put to an end with the arrival of the motor car, technological advances and a world of changing values.

The top postcard looks onto the bottom of the bridge road in 1912. Prestatyn's most glorious Victorian building is the Victoria Hotel, seen on the left, built in 1897 and is a striking testimony to the builders of the day. The building on the right is today the premises of Hedleys Interiors.

The men in naval uniform in the postcard above are from Arthur Aiston's troupe of Prestatyn Pierrots who entertained the visitors with their comic monologues, audience participation and song and dance routines on a stage with a piano on a sandy piece of land during those long hot summers in the early 1900s. The sandy piece of land is today the Nova's front car park.

It must have been a rare privilege and an impressive sight for those families on holiday from the industrial towns and cities to sit and watch the seaside Pierrots entertain and what precious memories to take home of a more glamorous and ageless time.

The bottom postcard is looking down Marine Road from the corner of Bastion Road in 1915 as one of Arthur Aiston's Pierrots, this time dressed in traditional pierrot's costume shares a joke with passers by. The building on the right was the National School, also known as the VP School (voluntary primary), opened in 1898.

The headmaster of the school was ET Williams who reminded the children each morning, "remember you were born in Prestatyn, poor, proud and pretty". He was to become mayor of Prestatyn in 1918. As chairman of the public health committee for Prestatyn Town Council during the 1920s, ET Williams composed this delightful verse, "If you are ill don't take a pill, I'll tell you something better still, for sunshine and air, weather that's fair and health giving rest, Prestatyn is best".

It ceased to function as a school in 1976. The old school is today the Suhail Indian Restaurant. The land on the left behind the ornate gas lamp became the site of the White Rose Motors Garage in 1928, the TA Centre stands here today. Gas lighting was introduced into Marine Road in 1901.

The fairytale princess in Rhyl

When Prince Charles and Princess Diana took an hour-long walk through Rhyl's High Street on October 27th, 1981, it was their first walkabout together since their wedding on July 29th, 1981, watched by an estimated TV audience of 700 million viewers worldwide. And it was Diana's first official visit – a trip to Rhyl.

Prince Charles had promised the people of Wales that he would bring the Princess to see them as soon as possible after the wedding. He kept his promise and Diana's pregnancy with William was announced shortly afterwards.

The day the Prince and Princess stepped from the Royal Rolls Royce at Rhyl, blue skies, brilliant sunshine and a bitterly cold wind greeted them, but this did not impair the warmth of welcome from the estimated 8,000 onlookers who had assembled along the High Street and promenade.

The Prince and Princess were observed to be evidently impressed by the cheering public and flag-waving school children who had come to see them.

Among the massed crowds with his camera was Arthur Dilks of Prestatyn who took the intoxicating colour photographs of Diana pictured here and has kindly donated copies of them for my archives. Arthur said, "Although there were crowds lining the High Street, I managed to take some close-up shots of Diana as she walked past. She looked towards me as if to shake my hand. I hesitated – I didn't know whether to put my camera down or shake her hand but I decided to carry on taking photographs".

"Diana looked so lovely in her dark pleated skirt and top under her bright red jacket and matching hat. I remember thinking how young and radiant she looked. Charles was walking on the other side of the street and I managed to take a superb picture of him too. It was wonderful to see the Princess at that time of her life – she had changed so much as she became older. But there was no doubt she was happy that day in Rhyl", Arthur added.

Of the many school children to greet the royal couple were the Rhyl High School Band who had earlier welcomed the Prince and Princess with the rendering of Men of Harlech. Among those who experienced this memorable day was Jonathan Fisher of Rhyl, who had been waiting since 8am and was told by Diana " I would have a jolly good lunch later if I were you".

David Batchelor of Rhyl who shook hands with Diana, who told him " what a terrific welcome – I will have to come here more often". At that moment someone shouted "Croeso i Gymru Diana". The Princess stunned those nearby and brought a cheer when she replied in Welsh "Diolch yn fawr". Walter Mills, of the Clwyd Multiple Sclerosis Society, whose wheelchair was colourfully decorated, was approached by Diana and who asked him how long he had been waiting and if he was cold. He later said she was so lovely, he cried.

To the shouts of Charles and Diana, the royal couple gave one last wave as they entered the royal car and onto the next engagement of their very busy North Wales tour. At Prestatyn they left hundreds disappointed as the royal car passed along the Coast Road without a stop. Bodnant School in Marine Road had been decorated with flags and bunting.

More than 200 pupils, children and adults waited for over half an hour to catch a fleeting glimpse of the royal couple. Headmistress Mrs Thomas was sad to say that the royal car passed so quickly.

Opposite and above : These intoxicating photographs of Diana show her on her first official visit – a trip to Rhyl in 1981, taken by Arthur Dilks of Prestatyn who stood among the crowds in Rhyl High Street. An indelible memory of the day he photographed a fairytale princess.

The days when we all knew one another

One of the characteristic and alluring features of Prestatyn throughout the 1800s and early 1900s were these delightfully picturesque thatched-roofed cottages that adorned the High Street.

The cottages seen here in 1905 stood on the corner of High Street and Meliden Road (the Catalogue shop is here today). The postcards pictured here capture in striking detail a less hurried, tranquil, elegant and graceful period in time, brought vividly to life with the horse-drawn vehicles and the well-dressed ladies on their bikes.

In the days when the London and North Western Railway steam engines pulled carriages that contained photographs above the seats of pretty towns to visit extolling the virtues of this premier line, photographs of Prestatyn were regularly featured showing these old cottages and described by the railway company as "Romantic houses in Prestatyn".

These cottages were inhabited when candles and paraffin lamps were used for home lighting and coal was used for heating and cooking. Subsequently, complaints were frequently made about the residents of the cottages throwing waste-water out into the streets and of chimneys catching fire causing the street to be constantly filled with smoke and soot.

Throughout the time people lived in the cottages, they consisted of irregular stone floors, narrow window space that admitted the minimum light, they were lacking in sewer connections which meant outside toilets, and due to coal fires in the cottages, large ash heaps collected at the rear of the buildings.

In time, the roofs became dilapidated and were declared unfit for human habitation by the medical officer who knocked the romance out of these "Romantic" cottages.

The still fondly remembered and very popular Savoy Café was built where these cottages once stood in 1919 (see page 37 of my book Memory Lane, Volume II).

Glady Parnell, an old resident of Prestatyn, sadly no longer with us, recalled in her memories some years ago, "Even to this day, I speak of Prestatyn as "the village".

Prestatyn of the Past.　　　　　Burrows' Series Prestatyn.

"I was born in the High Street and I can look back to a street full of life and characters. It was filled with rural activity from early morning when the clip-clop of a horse-drawn cart brought mail from Rhyl, you could set your watch by its regularity".

"In those days, we all knew one another in Prestatyn and the street was the scene of chatter and gossip. You could stand in the middle of the road which was unmade, very muddy in the winter, and dry and dusty in the summer, and recount some story or other without the fear of being knocked down as the pony and trap and bicycle were the only mode of transport. Such tranquillity is hard to imagine in this day and age".

The ornate horses drinking trough seen on the postcard on the opposite page was erected in 1881 when the High Street first obtained its own water supply. This trough can today be seen outside Pendre Gardens at the top of town. It bears the inscription "Praise God from whom all blessings flow, presented by two sisters in memory of living friends".

Fred Hobbs of Prestatyn told me that the two sisters were possibly Ethel and Bertha Hickson, wealthy sisters who were attributed to Pendre Private School in Fforddlas being built in the early 1900s.

Above: One of the more pleasant features of old Prestatyn were these thatched roof cottages that could be seen lining the High Street and were often described in the guide books of the time as "the romantic houses of Prestatyn". The ones seen here are pictured in the early 1900s and were located where the Catalogue shop is today at the top of the High Street. In the end, they became unfit for human habitation.

The end of a retail era

April 2nd 2005 saw the end of an era with the closure of one of Rhyl High Street's illustrious shops when possibly the town's oldest surviving family business closed its doors for the last time. After 120 years of successful trading, when Robert Scott, the great-grandson of the firm's founder, decided to take a well-earned retirement.

William Roberts' garden centre and pet food supplies which traded for 80 years on the corner of High Street and Brighton Road, was established in 1885 as a coal, corn and seed merchant and hay and straw dealer.

The Roberts family lived above the shop and it was during these early years that a member of the family became seriously ill and was confined to their bed, which overlooked the nearby Vale Road Bridge. On the doctor's advice, he requested that the bridge be closed to horse-drawn vehicles as the noise echoing from them as they crossed the bridge was unsettling his seriously ill patient, who thankfully later made a full recovery.

As the business grew, William Roberts purchased larger premises across the road in 1925, which was previously the Villiers Hotel and a Cocoa House for the Temperance Society (see page 44 of my book Memory Lane, Volume 2). William Roberts continued trading in coal, corn and seed at these new premises which developed into a garden centre and pet food supplier. Their old premises at 1 Brighton Road was later converted into the Odeon Cinema which was opened on October 30th, 1937, The Apollo bingo hall stands here today.

Apart from their shop in the High Street, the coal business traded from premises at their head office in Morley Road, where they controlled their own railway siding obtaining coal from Point of Ayr Colliery and pits in Lancashire and the Midlands. William Roberts delivered their coal known as "Rhylliance" coal by horse and carts to a large number of customers, mostly farmers, along the Vale of Clwyd.

Robert Scott, the last in line of the William Roberts family, has sold the property in High Street, relinquishing their 120 year reign of loyal service to the town and therefore firmly establishing the name of William Roberts in the pages of Rhyl's history books.

The William Roberts premises is today divided into two shops and continued under the new owner as a pet and fuel store, with the other half of the shop (known as Shipley Street - the original name for Brighton Road), selling gifts and furniture.

Opposite page: William Roberts' coal, hay and straw dealers at their premises in Brighton road pictured in the early 1920s. It was here that the business was established in 1885. The Roberts family pose for this photo showing William Roberts' wife Mary and their children, Llewelyn, Adina, Doris, Stanley, Jack, Edith, and the twins Maude and Hilda.

Above: William Roberts

Right: Robert Scott, last in the line of the William Roberts family who ran the shop for many years until its closure in 2005 is pictured in the doorway of his shop in the year of closure.

Gift to community remains a treasure

One of the finest stone-built community centres in the area with a history as notable as the village, is the building known as the Gronant Institute. Here is a potted history of this elegant building.

Built out of Gwespyr stone, it was opened, on September 20th, 1924, by Richard Hughes at a cost of £10,000, with £2,000 invested to provide some income for its upkeep.

Richard Hughes, a ship owner in Liverpool was the youngest of nine children belonging to Jane and Joseph Hughes, owners of the Gronant Inn, who also had a shop and bakery in the village and were also general carriers and partners in agricultural machinery hiring.

Richard Hughes left school at 14 and worked in a shipping office in Liverpool as a clerk. His inherited business instincts led him in 1884 to establish his own shipping company with financial help from his family.

His first of 42 ships, the Primrose, was launched in 1885 and his fleet increased, most had his favourite flower tagged to their names – Wild Rose, Moss Rose, and during the First World War, French Rose, Jellica Rose, with Prestatyn Rose being launched at the time of the opening of the Gronant Institute in 1924.

For years it had been Richard Hughes' wish to contribute something to his village and this culminated in the construction of the Gronant Institute and what he hoped would be a cultural and leisure centre. He bore the total cost of the building, furnishing and equipment, down to the cutlery and crockery.

The assembly hall was built to accommodate 400 people, with adjoining rooms intended as a library, reading room and a service kitchen. A full-size billiard table was provided and a stage erected for the performance of concerts and plays. Another room held the bowls equipment for the crown green in front of the building with seats furnished for spectators.

The war memorial was provided by public subscription and unveiled by Richard Hughes' daughter Dorothy who herself drove an ambulance throughout the First World War. During the Gronant Institute's opening, Richard Hughes said that the Institute must be free from partiality to any sect or denomination, non-political and must not be used for gambling or the selling of alcohol.

In later years, with the help of fundraising, grants and hours of voluntary work, the trustees have installed electricity, replaced the bowling green with a car park, improved the access, re-roofed the Institute, re-sited the war memorial, and the green rooms behind the stage have been made into a modern and up-to-date meeting room.

The five great grandchildren of Richard Hughes are now the freeholders of the Gronant Institute and other close members of the family still live in the village nearby. Richard Hughes left a lasting legacy that will forever be a memory of a man who had a great affection for his village. The hard-working Gronant Community Association, aims to raise the profile of Gronant by undertaking new and exciting projects in the village to remind people of its proud and valuable history and heritage.

Top photo: So elegant - The Gronant Institute pictured after its opening in 1924.
Bottom photo: A china beaker commemorating the opening of the Gronant Institute which was given to every child in the village.

Snapshots from Gwespyr's past

This Memory Lane focused on a picture gallery of people from the close-knit village of Gwespyr.

Photographs of people who were once familiar faces in a town or village hold considerable interest to readers who take great delight in recognising faces from the past who may have been a friend, relative, workmate or next door neighbour.

The older generation seen on the bottom photograph, as with every town and village, hold a valuable link to living history and retain that special magic to transport us back through time to tell us of a world of different thoughts and values, a world our grandparents and great-grandparents knew, the people, shops, buildings and the streets and avenues that were part of their everyday lives.

The older generation in our community, are of an invaluable benefit and are to be respected in high esteem.

But with the fading years our only passage to what many consider were better times are the memories contained in the photographs we posses and the engaging and inspiring anecdotes from the elderly people in our community.

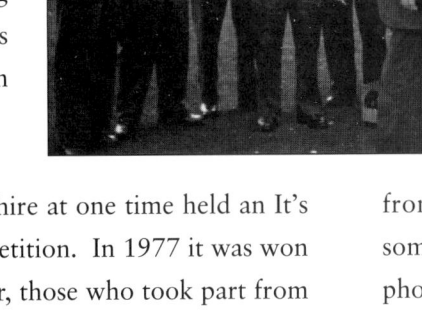

The old county of Flintshire at one time held an It's a Knockout village competition. In 1977 it was won by the village of Gwespyr, those who took part from the village are proudly pictured holding their trophy in the top photograph.

They are, back row L-R: Bryn Jones, Barry Faulkener, John Larner, Steve Whitelamb: front row L-R: Lesley Bonus, Judith Polem, Joyce Jones, Carol Whitelamb, missing from the photo are Vincent Price and David Hockney.

Pictured on the bottom photo are the merry men of Gwespyr on a day's outing in the late 1950s.

L-R: Lawrence Jones, John Roberts, Tom Jones, Joe Faulkner, Roger Williams, who ran the village post office, Wil Lloyd, Eifion Faulkner, David Watkins of Watkins Coaches, Meliden.

As a child growing up in Gwespyr, Wil Lloyd in this photo was known as 'Wil Brown Cow.' When I was about 12, I recall passing him one day and saying to him, "hello Mr Brown Cow". Not being known as a man who took kindly to a joke, he later mentioned what I had called him to my parents which resulted in what I thought was an unjust chastisement.

Sadly everyone in this photograph has since passed away. It can therefore, be reliably said that the photographs we posses hold happy memories of better times and the not so happy ones as well.

Each person staring at us from a photograph is a relative of someone, somewhere living in our community. If these photographs had something to say it would be this: "this is me, I was here, I existed."

Making of Prestatyn

PRESTATYN GOLF CLUB.—An "At Home."

The history of playing golf at Prestatyn, one of the most popular sporting pastimes in Prestatyn and the neighbourhood, dates back 100 years.

Prestatyn's first golf course was laid out by funding from Lady Mclaren in 1896. Lady Mclaren was the wife of Lord Aberconway and the daughter of Henry Pochin, one of Britain's foremost industrialists who went on to develop Prestatyn into a modern and up-to-date town.

The newly laid golf links were said to be the finest in Wales and were formerly opened in 1897 with a "Grand Golf Tournament".

Prestatyn's Golf Club was formed in 1905 when four Prestatyn residents are said to have had a meeting to discuss how the club should be formed. They did this by placing an advert in the Prestatyn Weekly, asking for those who were interested to attend a public meeting at the town's council chambers on July 10th, 1905.

Subsequently, an authority on laying golf courses was consulted and three possible sites were looked at for the building of a club house. After considering the sites, land in Barkby Avenue was designated and following a meeting with the owner of the land Mrs Mclaren, she agreed to let the site on a 10-year lease – the first five years at £5 per annum and the second five years at £10 per annum.

The grazing tenant T Lloyd Ellis of Penisardre Farm at the bottom of the High Street was also to be paid compensation of £20 a year (Penisadre Farm was located where the shopping precinct is today. It was demolished in 1964). The official opening of Prestatyn's first golf club house took place on October 11th, 1907.

Lady Mclaren remarked on the day : "The Golf Club would be the making of Prestatyn". The Golf Club house, which stood in Barkby Avenue opposite to the entrance of where Pontin's Holiday Camp is today, was a primitive-looking building, built of wood with a corrugated iron roof, which comprised a committee room, assembly hall, kitchen and dressing rooms with lockers. Refreshments, including

GOLF HOUSE FROM THE LINKS, PRESTATYN.

alcohol, were also available following a days golf.

Subscriptions for the first 100 members were one guinea (£1.05p) and Charles Mclaren was elected the club's first president. Later, strong feelings were expressed by the council against Sunday play.

In later years, when more modern and larger premises were required, a lease was taken on Stradbrooke House which the Trustees of Prestatyn Estates were converting into a residential golf house with an 18-hole course on the land between Barkby Avenue and Bastion Road.

Opened in 1926, a 1930s visitors' guide to Prestatyn remarked; "Prestatyn is known far and wide for its golf. The large white building of continental appearance on the sand dunes is the golf club headquarters and also a modern hotel".

"The course stretches for over a mile and offers delightfully springy turf, tricky holes over sand dunes and water courses, making the golf most enjoyable.

The 18th hole is played appropriately under the golf club's balconied windows and the floodlit appearance at night is one of the most spectacular sights in Prestatyn".

George Formby's father also called George was also a famous comedian of his day, suffered ill health through a chest complaint and became a frequent visitor to Prestatyn's Golf Club House as nothing gave him as much relief as sitting on the sandhills nearby, inhaling the fresh ozone-filled air from the sea.

The Golf Club House later became known as the Grand Hotel. Its name has been changed today to the Beaches Hotel. The present Prestatyn Golf Club, opened in 1971, is located off Marine Road East.

Opposite: Prestatyn's very first golf club house, opened in 1907, is pictured here in 1908 as golf club members attend an afternoon tea which was held each year by Lady Aberconway seen on the photo dressed in white.

Above: Prestatyn Golf Club House and Hotel pictured here in the 1920s. Today it is known as the Beaches Hotel.

Potted history of the old Crosville

Crosville Motor Services were at one time renowned for their public transport in North Wales and every person who ever made use of public transport in those days travelled by the familiar green colour of the Crosville bus. Here is a potted history of Crosville.

George Crossland Taylor and his brother James were early entrepreneurs with an interest in everything mechanical and electrical. George who was always refered to as Crossland bought two cars in 1906 built by the French company Morane, afterwards renting a warehouse in Chester with the purpose of assembling and selling French-designed cars.

It soon became apparent that more capital was needed and George eventually persuaded his French businessman friend Georges de Ville to invest in the company.

Subsequently, the new company Crosville Motor Company Ltd was created in 1906, the name being a combination of Crossland Pond de Ville, but, although the car making activities ceased in 1908, the company subsequently limited its operations to agency work and repairs.

In 1909, it was suggested to George Crossland by the then Crosville office manager Jack Morris that the company should consider providing a bus service between Ellesmere Port and Chester due to the indirect rail link. In 1910, Crosville approached Chester City council to request permission to start the service, which was later granted. Difficulties in communications and the purchase of a German wagonette meant that a large capacity Crosville car and a second-hand charabanc had to be used.

By 1913, the company was making a small profit and new vehicles were ordered to replace the varied collection of vehicles owned. Crosville inaugurated its first excursion into Wales in 1919 with a circular service taking in Mold, Hawarden, Queensferry, Connah's Quay, Flint and Northop. Flintshire was one of the more populated regions and Crosville saw this as a potentially profitable area for expansion. As a result, they built their routes to cover North and Mid-Wales, but these early vehicles were slow, often reaching speeds of only 12mph.

However, as motor transport developed, so did Crosville's fleet of buses reaching one hundred vehicles in 1933 with their largest depot at Mold Road, Wrexham.

Crosville's colours went through two changes before the familiar green. In 1928, the buses were painted grey before changing to red in the 1930s. When war broke out, a shortage of red paint meant that they were forced to use green, which was plentiful. The new image stuck and Crosville made it their permanent colour.

The promenade service at Rhyl was started by Brookes Brothers Motors whose business was bought by Crosville in 1930. As business improved in the summer, Crosville painted their Rhyl promenade bus service with cream paint as the buses looked more prominent and pleasant and quite unique, which was always an attraction to the public. The illustrious Crosville name disappeared from the roads of North Wales as part of a £2 million revamp, which saw the name replaced by Arriva in 1997.

Opposite: Crosville summer service on Rhyl prom opposite Woolworths in 1956. Its stops were; Marine Lake, Kinmel Bay and Winkups Camp.

Above: Crosville Rhyl promenade service bus standing at Rhyl bus station in 1938 (where the bus station is today in Rhyl). The building in the background is the Odeon Cinema, William Roberts can be seen on the left.

Discovering parts of the haunted town

In 1975, Barry's five year old son ran out of his home in Sandy Lane, Prestatyn, calling out to his parents, "Mum, Dad, there's a strange-looking girl sitting on a chair in the front room". But she wasn't an ordinary looking girl. What Barry's young son had seen was the ghostly figure of a young Victorian girl in period dress.

Barry and his family were returning home from having a day out and his young son, who had run on ahead, was the first to enter the house when he saw the "girl". She was about nine years old and dressed in what was later discovered to be Victorian style dress, sitting silently and motionless in one of the chairs in the front room. As his parents came through the door the ghostly figure of the young girl unexpectedly disappeared.

This was one of the many sightings of the young girl's ghostly figure that had been seen in different parts of the house, by every member of the family. Barry had seen her on two occasions in the kitchen. On the first occasion the ghostly little girl's figure had just stood there staring in an effort to pass through a door that was no longer there.

Perhaps the reason for this was that Barry had recently renovated the kitchen, and in doing so had covered up an old doorway that had been there since the house was built. Was the ghostly figure of the little girl looking to go through the doorway that she would never find?

In another sighting, Barry and his wife were sitting on the settee in the front room when they both saw her pass the kitchen door. She was also seen on the stairs by Barry's wife, who was on the telephone at the time. Barry's eldest son had also seen her in the back bedroom on a rocking chair holding a newspaper, he recalls that, "she had some kind of mist surrounding her".

The family have never felt intimidated by the appearance of the benevolent young girl's ghostly figure as there was never any harm inflicted, although they are mystified as to who or what she is and where she came from.

Barry recalls that "she" always makes an appearance when I am making alterations to the house, especially when there's a lot of banging. The last sighting of the young Victorian girl's ghostly figure was when Barry was pulling up the old staircase. He remarked that there will be many more alterations made to the house and no doubt many more sightings of this mysterious little girl's ghostly figure. Does the answer to this mystery lie in the previous owners of the house Barry surmises!

Above: Sandy Lane, Prestatyn, where alterations made to a house here were followed by the sightings of a young Victorian Girl's ghostly figure.

Postcards bring happy memories

Prestatyn's gardens and hillside shelter feature held a very pleasant and poignant surprise for Memory Lane reader Janet Ottley of Rhyl, in that her great-grandfather, Joseph Lloyd who opened Prestatyn's hillside shelter, was pictured on the postcard following the opening of the hillside shelter in 1929 (see next page).

The hillside shelter, with a jaw dropping panoramic view from its balcony, was donated to the town by wealthy local businessman, JF King of Stoneby Drive.

The honour of the shelter's opening was given to Prestatyn's oldest resident who was 79 year old Joseph Lloyd, a well known figure in the town, who opened the shelter by cutting a ribbon across the entrance to the shelter watched by a small crowd of family, friends and local residents.

Janet told me that the family had never seen this postcard before of their great-grandfather following the opening of the shelter and didn't even know it existed.

Janet's father often told her of her great-grandfather opening the shelter, and heartfelty tells me he would have been very proud and happy to have seen this postcard but sadly he passed away in 2005.

In a lengthy and engaging conversation over coffee and having known each other from those exhilarating and memory inducing days at Prestatyn's Lido in the 1960s (that's another Memory Lane story!), Janet went on to tell me that her great-grandfather, Joseph Lloyd, was born in Tanrallt, Meliden in 1851, and later married Mary Hughes of Dyserth, having six children during their marriage – Ann, Ester, Mary, Ellen, Herbert and Leah.

Joseph Lloyd once worked as a butcher in St Asaph and later as a clerk in Prestatyn council and was still an active employee of the council when he opened the hillside shelter.

Joseph Lloyd, a history maker in his family has today firmly established himself in the pages of local history books. He passed away in 1936 and is buried in the family crypt at Meliden churchyard.

At the end of our illustrious meeting, I was more than happy to present Janet with a copy of the postcard showing her great grandfather to complete a valuable and important gap to the family album's history of happy memories.

My deep rooted passion and fascination in local history is readily understandable when you discover rich and colourful human interest stories such as this.

Every old picture postcard undeniably tells a story and are vital chronicles of our history and heritage.

A family portrait: Back L-R, William Lloyd Ottley (Janet's father), Elen (Janet's grandmother and Joseph Lloyds daughter), Joseph Lloyd. Front L-R; Dorothy Mary Ellen, Herbert – Joseph Lloyds grandchildren. This photo was taken in 1915, Joseph Lloyd died in 1936 and is buried at the family crypt in Meliden churchyard.

On a summer's day in Prestatyn

Prestatyn's Coronation and Pendre Gardens along with the hillside shelter are integral to the town's history, heritage and character and the undisturbed serenity of the gardens and the shelter during the summer have been enjoyed for many years by visitors and locals alike.

On a warm, sunny, summer's day, the gardens and shelter have a peace and quiet quality that makes them an ideal retreat to relax and spend a few hours indulging in the reading of a book with a sandwich and a flask of coffee or to reflect upon your thoughts while watching the world go by.

Coronation Gardens in Station Road was at one time land that belonged to the poor of the parish and was to be used as allotments, but due to the unsuitability of the ground to grow anything, was bought by the council who developed the site and subsequently opened as Coronation Gardens in 1911 to commemorate the Coronation of Queen Mary and George V.

The opening ceremony was performed by John Pritchard, the oldest member of the Town Council, who unlocked the gates of the gardens with an inscribed silver key.

Part of the day's celebrations saw the town decorated with bunting, a street procession of shop-keepers horse-drawn vehicles, decorated floats on which sat Prestatyn's Rose Queen and her retinue which were all led by the accompaniment of Gwespyr Brass Band, the parish church bells were also rung for the day.

Later in the day, the schoolchildren of Prestatyn assembled at the Town Hall for tea (today's Scala Cinema buildings), where they each received a coronation mug, while the elderly of Prestatyn's over 60s, were presented with a coronation tea canister containing half a pound of tea.

In 1912, a new shelter was built at Coronation Gardens and opened when a ribbon surrounding the shelter was cut to the playing of Rhyl Brass Band. Recently, £25,000 was spent on renovating the old

THE PARK, PRESTATYN

shelter and installing new lighting to the gardens and the renovated shelter will be opened in December 2005.

Pendre Gardens on the corner of Fforddlas and Gronant Road were opened in 1951, a corner of the gardens is dedicated to those men who fell in the two world wars. A useful shelter once stood in the gardens, presented to the Town Council in 1953 by Councillor Eleanor Evans, who became Prestatyn's first lady mayor in 1939. Sadly the shelter had to be demolished due to irreparable damage from vandalism.

In 2004, a two-globed Victorian style lamp and plaque was erected at Pendre Gardens dedicated to our dear friend Sonia Hobbs. The plaque bears the words "erected in memory of Sonia Hobbs, her presence illuminated every occasion".

When the town was filled with summer visitors, their enjoyment was enhanced with a walk up to the hillside shelter to relish the jaw dropping and breathtaking panoramic view from the shelter's balcony.

The shelter was donated to the town by wealthy local businessman JF King of Stoneby Drive and was opened in 1929 by Prestatyn's oldest resident, 79 year old Joseph Lloyd who cut a ribbon across the entrance to the shelter.

A stone sundial was later given as a gift, to the hillside gardens below the shelter by Councillor T Pennant Williams who became mayor of Prestatyn in 1925, 1926 and 1937.

In 1977, comedian Derek Nimmo presented the hillside gardens with a seat in memory of Mrs Mason of Prestatyn who took him in as an evacuee during the war.

Opposite: Prestatyn's oldest resident, 79 year old Joseph Lloyd, is pictured with crowds at the hillside shelter following the cutting of a ribbon to the opening of the shelter in 1929.

Above: Coronation Gardens in 1927, were opened in 1911 to commemorate the coronation of Queen Mary and George V. The Victoria Hotel can be seen in the background.

The tranquil and unhurried days

Rhyl's Wellington Road, once known as Quay Street, reeks of the past in these early views and captures tranquil and unhurried days, and a more contented and innocent way of life as the Town Hall dominates the skyline.

The postcard on the opposite page is looking down Wellington Road towards the High Street from the corner of Elwy Street in 1905. A solitary horse-drawn vehicle in the distance treasures the pleasure of a deserted road as it approaches Elwy Street. There is a non-stop flow of blustering traffic passing through here today.

The building on the left displaying the Hovis sign was W Davies, the grocers. HSS Hire Shop and Walker's Store stand here today. Next door is the Liverpool Arms which has a link with Liverpool's old Walton jail in that the stone from this prison was used in the buildings at the rear of the pub, hence the pub's name.

It was between the Liverpool Arms and the gable-ended brick building that Sidoli's was later established in 1910.

The photograph above is an evocative insight into Rhyl's Wellington Road way of life in 1910. Kerfoot Hughes ironmongers, on the right also sold and hired bikes and bassinets (prams). This building is today occupied by P A Thomas and Son, jeweller and giftware, Beresford Adams Estate Agents and the Nationwide.

The construction of the Town Hall of granite and stone from the Graig quarries was started in 1874 by the Rhyl Improvement Commissioners, (the forerunners of the town council), as an administrative base for the then growing town.

In late 1874, James Taylor, chairman of the Improvement Commissioners, laid a foundation stone near the doorway of what later became the entrance to the Carnegie Free Library.

At a cost of £8,000, the town hall was opened in 1876. the opening ceremony was a colourful affair with the streets decorated in bunting with most of the shops closed and a procession led by two bands that proceeded along the promenade.

The Carnegie Free Library was opened in 1907 through the support of a £3,000 donation from an application to the trust of multi-millionaire Andrew Carnegie by Rhyl Town Council.

In those days, the reference and reading rooms at the library became the most important part of the building with an impressive 29 weekly papers and 15 monthly magazines.

To qualify to be a member of the reading library, you had to be over 10 years old, and no one under the age of 14 was allowed in the reference room without the appropriate permission from the librarian.

As early as 1898, pioneer cinematographer Arthur Cheetham was showing films every month at the town hall, films he filmed himself of local events in Rhyl and North Wales which included, E H William's Merrie Men on Rhyl Sands, a football match at Rhyl, Rhyl Town versus the Amateurs, Rhyl May Day, Irish mail train passing through Rhyl station, ladies boating at Aberystwyth Bay, the Duke and Duchess of York at Conwy, a street scene in Wrexham, a horse fair at Llangollen, and a Minstrel Show at the Happy Valley, Llandudno.

Arthur Cheetham later moved to Los Angeles with the purpose of becoming a film director. His films have survived to this day, leaving the town of Rhyl with an invaluable heritage of vintage local films.

Above: Looking down Wellington Road, once known as Quay Street towards the High Street from the corner of Elwy Street in 1905.
Opposite: Wellington Road in 1910, with the town hall dominating the skyline.

When summers were hot and dry

Gwynedd Parry, a once well-known figure in Rhyl, was president of Rhyl History Club during the 1980s. His vast knowledge of Rhyl's history along with Joe Jones (author of Rhyl and Roundabout as well as Rhyl: The Town and its People) was unsurpassed, and his fascinating slide shows and talks on the history of the town were in popular demand by local history groups, clubs and organisations.

Sadly no longer with us, he left these thought provoking memories of his early days in his families grocers business in Rhyl High Street in 1904, an evocative insight prior to pre-packed food and the advent of supermarket shopping. I use his original words.

"At the commencement of a day's trading, we opened at 8 o'clock, the first job to be done was to mop the black and white square tiled floor, then bring in the bread in it's various shapes, plus the cakes from the bakehouse situated at the rear of the premises and set them out in the window. The bakehouse had coke fired ovens and the bakers started at 4 am in the morning".

"Bread, cakes and confectionery took up one side of the shop and the other side was occupied by the provisions, bacon, cheese, butter and related products".

"The butter arrived in two forms, the Irish made it in beautiful clean square tapered boxes lined with strong greaseproof paper, while Danish butter came in equally clean wooden barrels held together with wooden hoops which were knocked off with a hammer and the sides just fell apart, exposing the lump of butter (in the winter). In those days there was no thought of pre-packed butter, each customers order was cut from the large slab of butter using two "butter pats", one having a sharp edge for cutting, the other having one side ribbed to decorate the piece of butter as it was patted into the desired shape. Some customers wanted salty butter so common salt was scraped from a seven pound block and added to achieve the required taste".

"Bacon was delivered from the railway goods warehouse and four sides wrapped in hessian were brought by horse-drawn lorry, then trucked to the shop's back yard and opened".

"Each side would then be washed with very hot water before being hung up to dry, the rib bones would then be removed, sometimes in a complete sheet and sold for pot boiling flavouring. Before the advent of the hand operated bacon slicing machine, bacon was cut by knife".

"Cheese was delivered by Mr Nuttall, the cheese dealer, each cheese weighing from 20 to 40 pounds, and the grocer would sample each one with his cheese taster. Sugar was originally sold in cones made from "fruitcap", a thick paper which was glazed on one side and rough on the inside".

"Soap came in several forms – three pound bars of white soap, 12 ounce bars of Lifebouy, 11 pound packs of Crossfields carbolic soap, 12 ounce bars of Mother Skiptons soap and Lever's Sunlight soap bath brick for cleaning steel knives. Powdered soap for washing clothes comprised of Hudsons, Rinso and Omo".

"In a nostalgic mood when our thoughts drift back to earlier days, the memory is prompted to recall a miscellany of experiences which have more or less been forgotten such as waking up above the shop to the sound of the clip-clop of the horse-drawn water cart on a summer's morning, which ejected a spray of water on to the road to keep the dust down. In retrospect, all summers seemed to have been made up of hot dry days".

Above: W Davies family grocers, Wellington Road, Rhyl, is seen in 1910, next to the Liverpool Arms.

Opposite: Edward's family grocers, Vale Road, Rhyl, pictured here in 1914, resembled many family grocers of the day, selling similar produce to Parry's and many other family grocers in Rhyl at that time. A photograph of Parry's grocers shop was unobtainable.

Memories from the times of war

During the Second World War, there were many men and women in our towns and villages involved in civil defence. These included air-raid wardens, ambulance drivers, first-aid helpers, home guard and fire fighters. The most notable of these were the ARP wardens (Air Raid Precautions).

In September 1935, local authorities were encouraged to organise air raid precautions and in 1937, an air raid warden service was created. As a consequence, in September 1939, 1.5 million men and women had joined the emergency services as ARP wardens.

The main role of the ARP warden was to report the extent of bomb damage to the Control Centre, assess the local need for help from the emergency services, staff the air raid shelters, use their knowledge of their local areas to find and reunite family members who had separated in the rush to find shelter from the bombings, extinguish fires due to incendiary bombs, administer first aid and enforce the blackout rules.

Under the blackout rules which began on September 1st, 1939, everyone had to cover their windows with black material, this was to make if difficult for German bombers to find their target in the dark. Street lights were also turned off and speed restrictions came into force.

Traffic accidents were common as headlights had to be blackened out, and due to the darkness, pedestrians often tripped on kerb stones, twisted ankles and bumped into one another on the pavement.

The photograph opposite is of Gwespyr's lookout post, used during the First and Second World Wars. long since gone, it was located on an elevated mound on Tanrallt and Llanasa Road corner (also known as Rose Cottage corner) and manned during the Second World War by the Observer Corps and Home Guard who kept watch with powerful binoculars for enemy aircraft over the Mersey and the Dee Estuary. A battery of searchlights were also manned at Bryn Llystyn farm above the village.

Opposite: This photo is of the brave ARP wardens of Gwespyr pictured in 1940.
Back row: L-R on the ladder, John Roberts, Mr Ellison, Tom Wiltshire, Emyr Parry, Eifion Faulkener, A Evans (village post man), Joe Thomas (landlord Mason's Arms Pub, Gwespyr)
Middle row: L-R Mrs A Jones, Mrs Hughes, Mrs G Williams and Mr JE Conway.
Front row: L-R Mrs B Roberts, Mrs JB Thomas, Mr G Williams, JB Thomas (headmaster at Picton School, Gwespyr), Mrs Conway, Mrs Evans, sitting on the ground Ken Williams (retired headmaster of Bryn Hedydd School, Rhyl).

The only major incident to have happened in Gwespyr during the war was when a German bomber on its way home unloaded two bombs that landed in a field near a house at the end of the village known as Ty Coch, blowing it's windows out and killing a cow.

Above Gwespyr village lookout post manned during the Second World War by the Observer Corps and Home Guard and below the brave men and women ARP wardens of Gwespyr pictured in 1940. Does anyone recognise a relative among them?

Potted history of Salem bungalow

One of the most frequently asked local history questions about which I am often approached and have received letters about is regarding a bungalow that once stood on the sandhills near Rhyl Golf Course.

One such letter I received came from Mrs Jennie Street of Clive Avenue, Prestatyn who wrote saying, "I have been told by many different people of a cottage that once stood on the beach near Rhyl Golf Course. I have several books on Rhyl and Prestatyn, but can't find any information or pictures of this cottage or how it looked, have you any information you can help me with on this cottage?"

In reply to Mrs Street's and other people's questions and to fill a gap in our local history books, here is a potted history of the bungalow that once stood on the sandhills near Rhyl Golf Course.

Salem bungalow as it was known, was an unique black and white painted prefab building which stood on a concrete base on the edge of Rhyl Golf Course on the sandhills opposite Robin Hood Camp.

Salem was built and owned by Civil Engineer Alfred Dickenson, who bought the land to build Salem from Bodrhyddan Estates in 1915 for the princely sum of £135.

A beautifully built verandah at the rear of Salem was also embellished with a rooftop balcony encircling part of the building capturing breathtaking views of the hills of Prestatyn, Meliden and beyond and also the great expanse of the sea. The owner relished in watching for the passenger steamers arriving and departing along the pier at Rhyl. Halcyon days indeed with the only sound of the waves lapping up on the seashore.

Standing in its own grounds with beautiful green lawns either side, nearby was the gardener's cottage and a six-foot bricked wall which enclosed a well-kept garden of vegetables, fruit and roses.

Oak panelled walls were the striking feature of Salem's lounge, complimented with period furniture of bamboo.

Throughout the 1920s and 30s, Salem was lived in by a Dilys Johnson Smythe nee Smith, a Rhyl bank worker who later married insurance agent Alan Firth Mellor (uncle of Chris Mellor who today runs the White Lion Inn, Glan-yr-Afon).

Painter and decorator Mike Bloxham of Prestatyn recalls painting Salem in the 1940s and recollects that Salem was undermined by the sea and that Dilys Johnson Smythe abandoned the building in 1944 to live in a house known as Lonawlar in Splash Point.

Mike recalls that as a prefab building, Salem was taken down in pieces and rebuilt in another area. Mike also recalls that during the summer in the 1940s, a Rhyl donkey man kept his donkeys in the grounds of Salem for the purpose of donkey rides on the beach for the holiday makers.

Salem's brick garden wall and concrete foundation were eventually washed into the sea by strong waves and when the tide is out this can be seen on the beach opposite Robin Hood Camp today.

Opposite: A rare photograph of Salem bungalow pictured in the 1930s. It once stood on the sandhills opposite Robin Hood Camp and was undermined by the sea in 1944.

Above: Dilys Johnson Smythe nee Smith, who lived at Salem throughout the 1920s and 30s is pictured on the rooftop balcony of Salem. She had two daughters: Dilys and Irene.